SALESMANSHIP

Enterprise Manager's Guide

Wilfred Rachan

Order this book online at www.trafford.com
or email orders@trafford.com

Most Trafford titles are also available at major online book retailers.

Print information available on the last page.

ISBN: 978-1-4907-7116-8 (sc)
ISBN: 978-1-4907-7115-1 (e)

Library of Congress Control Number: 2016904019

Because of the dynamic nature of the Internet, any web addresses or links contained in this book may have changed since publication and may no longer be valid. The views expressed in this work are solely those of the author and do not necessarily reflect the views of the publisher, and the publisher hereby disclaims any responsibility for them.

Our mission is to efficiently provide the world's finest, most comprehensive book publishing service, enabling every author to experience success. To find out how to publish your book, your way, and have it available worldwide, visit us online at www.trafford.com

Any people depicted in stock imagery provided by Thinkstock are models, and such images are being used for illustrative purposes only.
Certain stock imagery © Thinkstock.

Trafford rev. 03/18/2016

 www.trafford.com

North America & international
toll-free: 1 888 232 4444 (USA & Canada)
fax: 812 355 4082

Salesmanship

Enterprise Manager's Guide

Important Note

The proceeds from the sale of this book will go to support Sugar Bell Foundation for Animal Care. Sugar passed away on March 5, 2014 in Singapore. She was 14 years and 7 months (human-age-wise, she was 102 years old). Sugar was a Maltese that believed she was a rottweiler. Adorable but aggressive, especially to the mail couriers, she was cute but at times cranky when kids touched her. She was a spoiled brat but was stellar whenever Kelvin Seow came to the house with nice treats for her. ☺

She will always be remembered and forever loved.

Acknowledgments

Thanks to my customers. You come first. Without you, this book would not have been possible.

Thanks to my fellow colleagues, past and present, for your many contributions, which were given both knowingly and unknowingly. I started this project in 2012, working in my private time. This project was born out of necessity as we had very little success in the recruitment and development of sales managers with the knowledge and practice of salesmanship.

Thanks to the management thinkers and writers before me, on whose shoulders I have stood (meaning they helped shaped my thoughts) so that I could complete my project on *Salesmanship: Enterprise Manager's Guide.*

Thanks to my mentor Wolfgang Horinek, for his detailed review of this book. His pointed questions set me thinking deeper on matters such as social media in sales, challenging the customers, and selection criteria shift in importance during sales cycle. His insights into the sales processes have certainly raised the quality of this book.

Thanks to Denice Lim for investing her private time to support my work with her creative selection and formatting of the illustrations used in this book. Her dedication and contribution have been invaluable.

Thanks to Nicole Anne Ee and Eugene Fletch, my two "paranymphs," for raising my curiosity about the future and what it holds. You have motivated me with a sense of our common academic obligation to help shape it.

Most importantly, thanks to my caring, loving, and supportive wife, Roslyn Ng. My deepest gratitude to you. Thank you for your encouragement when the times got tough. It is a great comfort and relief to know that you have been taking care of the heaps of home and other matters single-handedly while I relentlessly dispensed my time to complete this project.

Contents

Preface

Salesmanship: Enterprise Manager's Guide has been developed based on practical sales experience over the last two decades in the sale of capital goods for cargo handling and software applications for the improvement of operational performance. The book was born from the need to train and guide our sales managers. In the information age, it is no longer sufficient to hire salespeople with sales and marketing qualifications. There is a paradigm change in the function of sales in an enterprise.

On the one hand, the sales manager has to be transformed into an entrepreneur. On the other hand, the sales manager has to be trained to become a knowledge worker (i.e., an engineer and a problem solver). The sales managers need to think in terms of commitment and at the same time be able to comprehend and document the processes and workflow (i.e., supply chain and value chain) of a customer during his sales visits.

Salesmanship is about relationship management (i.e., relationship with internal and external customers, suppliers, contractors, agencies, etc.). Relationship brings us into politics. The sales manager needs to have situational awareness and be sensitive to the cultural factors present during a sales cycle and product-delivery process.

Salesmanship is about leadership (i.e., the capacity to translate vision into reality). The sales manager is motivated and guided by principles (i.e., he is a soldier and a gentleman). The sales manager being of strong character will be able to overcome adversity during sales without resorting to con schemes or misleading any customers.

The book is a summary of the practical sales knowledge and experience I acquired over the last twenty years.

Disclaimer
No gender discrimination intended for the practice of salesmanship.
The term *sales manager* used in this book refers to both male and female.

About the Author

Wilfred is currently the managing director of IS SEACOS Asia, based in Singapore. His main role and responsibility is in the sale of maritime software and services. Wilfred has been in sales function for the last twenty years.

Wilfred's main domain of interest is in supply chain synchronization (i.e., getting the right item in the right quantity to the right place). Having worked in the field of information technology since 1984, Wilfred is keen to seek opportunities to harness ICT (information and communications technology) to drive supply chain synchronization.

Wilfred has sales experience mainly in the sale of capital goods for cargo handling and software applications for the improvement of operational performance. Wilfred started his sales career after ten years with Nixdorf Computer, working on software and consulting on manufacturing solutions. He then spent another five years in container-handling-equipment sales for the Asia-Pacific market. Wilfred returned to sales by selling SAP software solutions for manufacturing companies. The last five years, he has worked in the sale of maritime solutions and services.

Wilfred has also taught part-time courses in Singapore at the German-Singapore Institute (now part of Temasek Polytechnic) on Material Requirement Planning (MRP) and Master Production Scheduling (MPS) and at Singapore Institute of Purchasing & Materials Management (SIPMM) on Enterprise Resources Planning (ERP).

Wilfred is listed on the Singapore *Who's Who - Industry Professionals Directory*.

Wilfred earned his PhD from Leiden University in the Netherlands.

Wilfred is married and has a daughter.

01. Introduction

> "Nothing happens until somebody sells something!"
>
> —Arthur "Red" Motley

Sales as a function in all businesses are pervasive throughout an organization. Although there are functional departments with a primary responsibility for sales, it is the goal of a business to sell and report revenue and profit.

"Salesmanship is the practice of investigating and satisfying customer needs through a process that is efficient, fair, sincere, and mutually beneficial, aimed at long-term productive relationship" (www.businessdictionary.com).

It is no longer enough to hire salespeople with sales and marketing qualifications. The salespeople usually have to be recruited from the technical department and trained to do sales. This will enable a sales manager to engage a customer's technical team with a degree of competency. This will ensure that a proposal put forth will be first technically sound and second commercially viable.

There is a shift in the sales process from a transaction-only buyer–seller relationship to a collaboration on framing a problem and then making a proposal for a solution. In this collaborative sales approach, unlike in the past, a sales manager has to interact with a customer's team quite intensively over a longer period of presales cycle. The envelope of participation in a customer's team by a sales manager is broadened and goes beyond the transaction-type-sales process. Further, this interaction will continue after the sales and into the delivery process and beyond.

This guide is an attempt to structure the sales function of a commercial enterprise toward the paradigm shift—from a buyer–seller relationship to a collaborative relationship of doing business. This shift dictates that the old style of sales will no longer be productive in sustaining sales and securing new customers.

This text is intended for the business managers and executives having sales and nonsales roles to give them a better understanding and appreciation of the challenges of sale making in the information age.

This text should also provide good guidance in the development of new hires for sales, marketing, and management roles.

For the experienced sales manager, this text will be a good revisit to the mind-set, methods, and means of the sales trade.

The guide should also provide a good text for students learning about sales, marketing, and management.

02. Landscape of the Business

> I have found in the course of my career that an awareness and study of
> people, history, and political issues, social and technological trends all lead
> to a better understanding of the dynamics of the marketplace.
>
> —Regis McKenna

The concepts of supply chain and value chain are fundamental to the understanding of the landscape in which a business is operating. Once he has mapped the supply chain (i.e., external-facing) and value chain (i.e., internal-facing), a sales manager can start making sense of the operating environment of a business. This approach enables the players and factors to be identified (i.e., partners, competitors, legal issues, compliance, safety, and others).

The sales manager needs a situational awareness of the business-operating environment before any attempt at problem solving can be initiated. One common approach to creating this situational awareness is by means of a SWOT analysis. The strengths and weaknesses of an organization are internal-facing and identify what are working and what need attention. The opportunities and threats are external-facing and alert the organization on what to focus its resources on and what risks need to be mitigated. During a SWOT analysis, the focus is always the prospective customer.

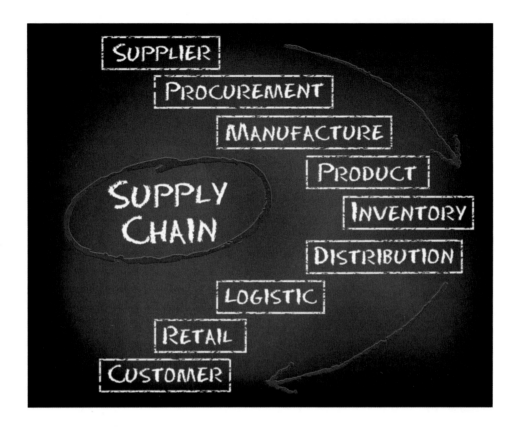

The sales manager needs to know his competition. What is the competition doing? What are their price points? What are their strengths and weaknesses? These will be useful during the lobby process to position products and services to the customer. The sales manager must always keep in mind that the competition is also not sleeping. They are also engaging in SWOT analyses and strategic marketing efforts. They will harness their network to get competitive data on you as you are doing on them. In the end, the key competition comes down to data or data processed to become information. When such information is used for competitive advantage, it is called intelligence. This is one reason why business intelligence and OLAP (online analytical processing) software have become significant.

Time is of key importance. Competitive information becomes obsolete and outdated in a short span of time. When decisions are based on obsolete and outdated information, the results can be detrimental to the business. Checks and balances need to be put in place to filter, segment, and authenticate the data being processed for sales decision-making. The sales manager must, on a daily basis, scan the landscape to see the movements/shifts in the activities of the competition.

The sales manager must also be aware of the people movement. When a sales manager moves from one competitor to another, what is the likely consequence, and will it provide an opportunity or create a threat to the sales pipeline? People are a key element in the network of business transactions. Relationships are important in maintaining and servicing accounts. Likewise, if we lose a team member to the competition, what will be the consequence?

The sales manager needs a good appreciation of the industry factors in which the customer's business is operating. This is an extension of the business landscape. This is knowledge about the macroeconomics that affects the business operations. The business is affected by the supply and demand and needs to remain viable as shifts in the industry put pressure on the business to drive further efficiency and reduce cost.

One possible way to acquire such knowledge is through the subscription to industry journals. Another is through participating in networking sessions. Take shipping as a simple example; on the demand side, it is affected by, for example, cargo (electronic-manufacturing industry), and on the supply side, it is affected by, for example, fuel (e.g., oil and gas industry). An increase in the price of bunker fuel will drive the need for higher efficiency and cost saving. The industry dynamics do not stay constant; a shift in one related industry will indirectly affect the industry in which the business operates.

Government initiatives to support the industry coupled with supportive legislation can provide the impetus for growth. For example, Singapore is a maritime hub resulting from government initiatives and supportive legislation. Many shipping companies have shifted their regional headquarters from Hong Kong to Singapore. Grants are available for companies operating in Singapore to defray the cost for investment to drive efficiency, productivity, and safety.

The sales manager also has to be familiar with knowledge of industry practices such as ISO (International Standards Organisation) to raise the standard of delivery whilst improving efficiency and productivity. Industry-regulation compliance and environmental standards, for example, emission control.

The product or services sales are not only about the product or service but also about the seven P's (i.e., product, price, promotion, place, physical evidence, people, and process). There is voluminous literature on this 7P's of the marketing mix on the web. Therefore it adds no value to indulge in a detail elaboration of the 7P's. The sales manager needs to start thinking about the product or service in terms of the 7P's. The 7P's, individually or in a mix, can offer the sales manager several different perspectives of the product or service that fit the customer selection criteria at the different stages of the sales cycle.

By defining a product or service in this broader scope, i.e. the 7P's against a backdrop of the "SLEPT factors" and studying the "supply chain" of the product or service, a picture of cross industry learning emerges. This cross industry learning ensures the survival of the sales manager in the current market conditions of intense competition and selling price decline.

03. Intense Market Competition

To be successful, you have to have your heart in your business, and your business in your heart.
—Thomas Watson Sr.

Sales is no longer simply selling products or services (i.e., as long as you have a good product, people will make a purchase). Today, there is intense market competition; chances are that you are one among several vendors competing to supply the same product or service. As markets mature, chances are also that you will encounter replacement/retrofit deals more than first-time installations.

Under the current market environment, prices (product prices, service rates, etc.) are always dropping and with them are the margin and profit levels. Competition drives the price down; therefore, one has to find new ways to become efficient and effective in delivery to try and bring the cost down as well to record a small margin and therefore profit for the sale.

It is not only the local competition that causes the price slide. Competition from emerging economics—like India, China, and other Asian countries—is even more worrying. Their cost of production and service delivery are much lower than, for example, in Singapore. New initiatives for the subdivision of production toward these lower-cost economies may become necessary to ensure the survival of the enterprise. Such decisions are sometimes beyond the scope of a sales manager. Mobilizing government grants/subsidies where applicable could be a good way to defray the cost of the project for the customer.

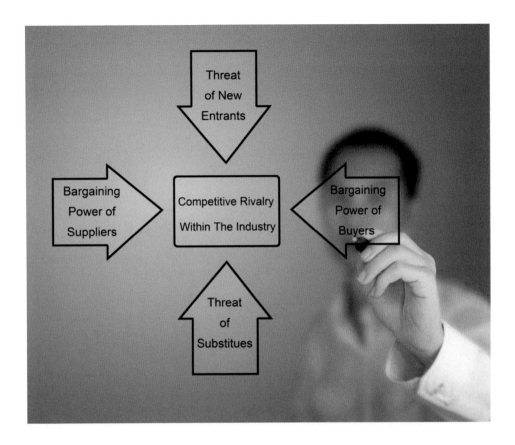

Quality is no longer a differentiator for sales. Quality is a given, and even products coming out of emerging economies are no longer of inferior quality. In fact, given their lower-cost model, competition from these economies can offer more in terms of service bundling.

However, local support and presence can be good sales arguments against this type of competition—provided they do not have a local operation. This has an impact on response time (due to the time difference or geography) and also communication (native language may not be English).

Developing payment terms and new financing initiatives for product/project financing can be a good differentiator. For example, converting CAPEX (capital expense) to OPEX (operational expense) allows flexibility to the customer. However, not all customers prefer OPEX. It depends on who is the budget owner (e.g., IT department) and who is the end user (i.e., operations department). In this case, the operations department will push for CAPEX.

Sales is no longer simply selling, and the sales manager can also no longer be just a sales manager. The sales manager has to transform himself into an entrepreneur.

How should the sales manager transform himself into an entrepreneur? The sales manager can start by *thinking like an entrepreneur*. The transformation can be achieved by "practice" on a daily basis. The sales manager must endeavor to deliver value, i.e. to exceed the customer's expectations. Og Mandino put it best, "Always render more and better service than is expected of you, no matter what your task may be." This is by no means an easy task and not all sales managers are able to make this leap (More on entrepreneurship in Chapter 28).

04. Conflict in the Organization

Life's problems wouldn't be called "hurdles" if there wasn't a way to get over them.

—Anonymous

Sales as a function is pervasive throughout an organization. A commercial enterprise is set up to fulfill a customer need. The start of this fulfillment process is the identification of the customer and his needs, and then you sell your product or service to satisfy those needs. The sales process does not end with the securing of a purchase order. It continues until the product or service is delivered and payment has been collected.

Therefore, multiple departments are involved at different stages of the sales process. Usually, the organization setup is function-oriented (i.e., accounts, sales, operations, etc.). These departments have their respective KPIs for performance measurement and rewards. During the sales process, this setup often creates a conflict of KPIs in the organization. It is common practice in most organizations to have a set of the following objectives:

a) Reduce product cost
b) Increase customer service
c) Reduce inventory
d) Increase asset utilization

These goals are obviously valid. However, this apparently innocent-looking set of goals creates a considerable set of conflicts within four major functional areas of the organization: production/delivery, sales, finance, and costing/controlling. Figure 1 illustrates these conflicting objectives.

A closer look at the enterprise's production/delivery-function performance toward the objectives would reveal that it is actually the ability to make long runs without breaking setups that is the primary requirement for the department to reduce product cost and increase resource/machine utilization. Naturally, this will require raw-material inventories in front of those long-running machines. However, as demands for customer service change, these long runs inhibit the ability of the company to provide all products to the customer when needed. Also, inventory is being built at the same time.

The sales function has the responsibility to maximize customer service, but in order to do so, they must have more finished inventory whenever required. This means shorter runs for the production department, along with higher product costs and even lower facility utilization.

The general accounting group in the finance department has a goal to reduce costs throughout the company. This requires an overall reduction of inventories from every department. It is easy to see the conflict this produces. Within the same finance department is another group (i.e., cost controlling) that is at direct odds with the general accounting group.

The goal of the cost controlling group is to reduce product cost, which inevitably forces the purchasing department to buy larger lots in order to get favourable discounts, which then reduces the unit-purchase cost for the inventory. At the same time, they want long runs from the manufacturing department for the same reason. Thus, if cost accounting was to have its way, product cost would drop and facility utilization would go up, but the inventory level would increase and the customer service would go down.

Fig. 1: Conflict of Objectives (Only the objectives in blue are achieved.)

Typical Functional KPIs of an Enterprise				
Enterprise (Goals)	Product Cost	Sales / Services	Inventory	Utilization
KPI (Settings)	⬇	⬆	⬇	⬆
Production / Operations	**Reduction in Product Cost**	Reduction in Customer Service	Inventory Buildup	**Improved Asset Utilization**
Sales	Product Cost Increases	**Improved Customer Service**	Reduction in Inventory	Underutilization of Asssets
Finance	Product Cost Increases	Reduction in Customer Service	**Reduction in Inventory**	Underutilization of Asssets
Costing/Controlling	**Reduction in Product Cost**	Reduction in Customer Service	Inventory Buildup	**Improved Asset Utilization**

Sales managers need to appreciate the causes of potential conflicts and be able to foresee and manage the pushback or uncooperative behavior of people from the other functions in the organization. Sales managers have to protect their customers from these negative experiences that may arise from their enterprises' other functional areas.

This is a balancing act to be performed by the sales manager as he keeps in mind the interest of the company and keeping the customers' demands harmonized with the constraints of the internal customers. The other functional teams are the internal customers of the sales manager. More often than not, the internal customers are more difficult to handle for the sales manager than the external paying customers.

05. Profile of a Sales Manager

Hire character. Train skill.

—Peter Schutz

Hard work is a given for the sales profession and is coupled with long hours. However, it is not working harder but working smarter that will give a winning edge in sales. The sales manager has to be willing to do things differently. In order to be successful in the application of the salesmanship based on the above definition, the sales manager will need to develop some prerequisite technical skills and behavioral traits.

Technical competency, among other skills, includes the following pertinent ones:

Effective Planner: The sales manager needs to be able to manage working with multiple customers whilst managing his own priorities. The sales manager needs to master the discipline of "starting with the end in mind" (i.e., thinking about what needs to be done before going ahead with it). Essentially, planning involves the competency to develop sales plans, identify potential customers, plan account strategies, and manage daily, weekly, monthly, and quarterly priorities and objectives.

Consultant: The sales manager needs to be able to learn from the current customers' processes and initiatives and develop the competency to know what will be applicable and workable for future potential customers. To reach this stage, the sales manager needs to have a deeper understanding of the potential customer's processes and business environment. It is no longer sufficient to sell features and benefits (FAB). The shift is toward identifying the problems, pains, and needs of the potential customer. Having identified the needs, the sales manager then makes a solution proposal to address those needs. So it is no longer about the sales pitch but more about organizing the presentations/demonstrations that are applicable for the particular customer. Each meeting or contact with the customer drives the relationship into a deeper collaboration.

Master Learner: The sales manager's ability to be an effective planner or knowledgeable consultant depends on his passion to learn, continuously improve his knowledge in the field, and expand his scope in practice. The sales manager can identify what are his weaknesses and strengths in the domain of knowledge. He can then improve by means of reading, attending seminars, or networking with others in the industry.

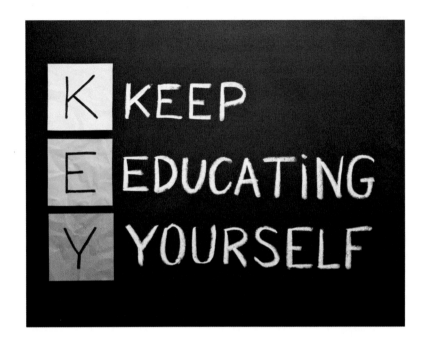

Behavioral traits, among other behaviors, include the following pertinent ones:

Perseverance: There are times when success is slow in coming. When I started in the sale of maritime-cargo solutions, it took one year before I was finally able to close a deal. During this first year, there were times, especially during the time I lost a deal that I worked on for months, I felt frustrated and demoralized and thought about changing jobs. I am happy that I persevered to achieve success. It is really the magic word for salesmanship to work. Never give up. See the next illustration. Many considered to be failures in life were people who did not realize how close they were to success when they gave up. In close relation to the topic of perseverance, the sales-manager faculties of adversity quotient (AQ), emotional quotient (EQ), and intelligence quotient (IQ) need to be developed. AQ is the measure of how one responds to adversity (i.e., challenges, rejections, and unexpected outcomes). This is a measure of one's optimism (i.e., mental attitude or worldview). EQ refers to the ability to recognize one's own and other people's emotions. IQ refers to the measure of human intelligence.

Friendly Disposition: A sales manager needs to be well attired, have a clean haircut, and have a good pair of clean shoes. This is the package the customer sees even before a word is said. The handshake should be firm, and the sales manager should maintain eye contact with a friendly manner. When the customer is talking, it is wise to respond with an encouraging nod to provide feedback that you are listening to what is being said. Never get yourself in an argument or confrontation with a customer—even if he is wrong. Especially in Asia, you need to give face (i.e., just let it go by first as a sign of respect). You can always come back and clarify the issue at the next opportunity, possibly under different circumstances (e.g., an individual meeting). The same applies for telephone calls, e-mails, and other written forms of communication.

Problem Solver: The sales manager with a problem-solving mind-set has a positive attitude in life as well. He does not see a problem; he sees an opportunity. All the advances we made in the world—all that we have achieved—were the results of problem solving. In business, some problems are known, and the customer will acknowledge a proactive search for a solution. Then there are also unknown business problems that the customer may not have identified as of yet. The customer's ignorance can be the sales manager's opportunity. However, efforts to create awareness may meet with a pushback from the customer's team. After finding and stimulating the need (i.e., need engineering), the sales manager can participate in the preference building, shaping of the issues, and structuring of the solution and entrench himself to secure the deal even if there has to be an open-tender bidding.

"It could be an expensive repair, or it could be just be the plug is out."

Communication: Interestingly enough, the general belief is that a sales manager must be someone who is a good talker and enjoys talking (i.e., a used-car salesman is a good example). Neil Rackham (*SPIN Selling*), in his findings, gives an interesting conclusion: the best salespeople are not necessarily the best talkers. They are the best listeners. Listen first. Find the need first, then present the solution (i.e., understand the problem/pain in detail first by asking questions and listening intently, and only after having understood the problem/pain in the context of the business environment do you offer solutions that are relevant and practical).

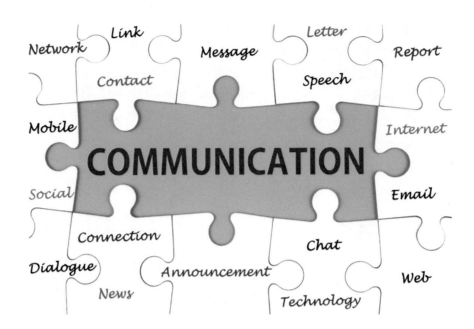

In the context of salesmanship, the sales manager has to develop his communication skills, i.e., verbal, written, behavioural, cultural, etc. The goal of communication for the sales manager is to get an *insight* of the customer's business processes. Having secured an insight, the sales manager uses Aristotle's "Ethos, Pathos and Logos" to construct a persuasive message that will position the product or service and move the deal toward a close (more on this in Chapter 11).

06. Understanding the Customer

You must originate and you must sympathize; you must possess, at the
same time, the habit of communicating and the habit of listening.
—Lord Beaconsfield

One of the key skills for a sales manager is the ability to *listen*. But listen to what? So listening is only one part of the key equation. Asking the right question and then listening with attention to the customer's response are critical. This behavior will enable the sales manager to collect the right data for the qualification of the sales lead and also to identify and structure create the solution that will fulfill the customer's needs.

Sometimes the customer will continue to talk. As soon as the sales manager realizes that the customer is indulging more time than he can afford in talk irrelevant to the sale and as soon as he has the opportunity, the sales manager will redirect the customer by asking the right questions. I hold the opinion that it is far better to hold a professional relationship with the customer than to allow the relationship to get too personal.

Customers are also operating under intense competitive-market pressures in their own fields. The problems they are trying to resolve are no longer single-factor problems. Today the problems are usually multifactorial and require a lot more thought at different hierarchy levels until you finally reach the root causes that need to be resolved. Then comes this question: Once the root cause is resolved, how can we prevent its recurrence in the future? The questions have to be structured to get the right details to frame the problem in the first place. Only when this has been done correctly can one expect a right solution.

Salesmanship provides the guidance to resist the temptation of talking too much about the functions and features of the product or service to the customer and hoping that the customer will, on his own, make the connections between the functions and features of the product or service to his own needs. Most of the time, the customer is unable to do so as this mapping from functions and features of the product or service needs a body of knowledge acquired through past learning and experience.

More often than not, the customer has no interest in the functions and features of the product or service. All he is keen to know is how to solve his current (and future) problems and achieve a competitive edge for his business. He wants to know how he can become effective and efficient in the delivery of his products and services. He wants to increase the volume of his business and thereby increase his profit. The sales manager has to invest time and effort to first understand the problem (which is usually complex) of the customer before attempting to solve the problem by simply and swiftly offering the product or service as a potential solution.

Bernard Baruch put it wisely: "If all you have is a hammer, everything looks like a nail." This is like that saying. If what you have is only a "hammer," then all problems appear to be solvable with a "hammer." Understanding the customer takes time. The sales manager needs to be patient and study the processes and workflow of the customer in some degree of detail.

Neil Rackham put it best with SPIN (situation, pain/problem, impact, and need). The sales manager must comprehend the situation of the customer; identify what are the pains (or problems) that he is facing. The sales manager must then map the identified pains to the impacts they have on the organization. From the impacts one derive the needs to resolve these pains. This is best achieved by the sales-manager skill of listening to the customer by asking the right questions.

The sales manager should not be too hasty to propose a solution. After having identified the needs, the sales manager should verify with the customer if his understanding has been right (e.g., Is it true that the team members from the customers are unanimous on the identified need?). Only after this is well documented should the sales manager and his technical team attempt to apply the solutions to the customer's needs.

07. Politics of Deal Making in Sales

> We live in a world in which politics has replaced philosophy.
>
> —Martin L. Gross

The key to success in sales today is having relationships. There is an abundance of literature on relationship marketing, so I don't have the need to elaborate on this. It will be sufficient to emphasize that for salesmanship, it is one of the main tasks of the sales manager to build and maintain relationships as his network of contacts is developed.

Ask any salesman and he will tell you that big sales are often very competitive and political. Ask any salesman to tell you how he plans to win such a sale. The response is usually naive to the extreme. Looking at sales as a whole, most sales managers do not think much beyond the next few calls that they are making in any detail. If they do think beyond, it is usually in terms of evidence. They will give examples of survey, user visit, demonstration, proposal-handover presentation, contract-terms negotiation, etc.

I believe that a better way of looking at sales as a whole is to list the various commitments that you wish to achieve. Create a flowchart on getting the customer to commit to small decisions. The decision box from flowchart diagramming is used to illustrate yes/no outcomes and the path forward. That is to list the various commitments that you wish to achieve. Typically, the plan might be as shown in appendix B, the exact calls being determined by circumstances. Let's have an example with an initial call to a chief executive officer (CEO). I want the CEO to write a memo saying "I can proceed with a survey" or "I can set up a meeting with the project team" to his staff. I want the CEO to set a decision date in a board meeting, commit to evaluate us seriously by coming for a site visit, or set a date for a board presentation of our solution. I want the CEO's staff to tell him that our solution is exactly what they need. I want the operations manager to tell the CEO that he needs our system. I want the CEO to sign the order.

Think in terms of commitments, not in terms of evidence. I think you will agree that this is far stronger. If any objective fails, you may have to replan, but you will have a far clearer direction by then. An account plan is a list of calls with only yes/no outcomes. This definition allows sales managers to judge the quality of the plan and very quickly establish resources to support the plan.

The method on winning politically that is described below is a slightly artificial mechanism. However, it does force you to consider the political influence at work, and it helps to plan the sale. You must ask yourself the following questions and try to answer them honestly.

a) Who will be there at the final decision-making meeting? Will it be a board meeting? Will it be a committee meeting? Will the recommender be there?
b) What will be the voting clout of each member (a number out of ten)? (Make a judgment call here.)
c) What people and how many must you have on your side if you are trying to ensure that you win? List their names.

Now we can convert the flowchart diagramming's decision diamond to if statements in the same way as we do when we are coding in a programming language:

a) "I can win politically *if* I can persuade the CEO that he really needs the system within three months."
b) "I can win politically *if* I can persuade the CFO that he really needs a good cash-management system."

You will win politically when you stop saying "If I can persuade them . . ." and you start naming individuals who count. Then the only important question that remains is, do we have a plan to influence the persons in the decision-making committee?

Recommending Committee				
People	Albert	Brian	Collin	Danny
Importance (out of 10)	5	7	6	9

Decision Committee				
People	Danny	Robert	Sarah	Timothy
Importance (out of 10)	5	7	5	3

08. Prospecting

Vision without action is a daydream. Action without vision is a nightmare.
—Japanese Proverb

It is the sales manager's job to start with the segmentation-decision-process output and convert the prospects list into a priority list for sales-call action. This is the beginning of the sales campaign's planning stage. The prospect list can be identified from sales directories, industry journals, existing customer referrals, newspaper classification ads, etc. Having identified the potential prospects, the sales manager should make an initial request for a meeting to understand the customer, not to pitch the sale of any product or service.

The sales manager needs to persuade the contact person/manager in the prospect's organization by using *consequence*. This the sales manager will do by documenting the key areas of activity and mapping the products/services that will be applicable to resolve the prospect's problems. The sales manager should resist his hurried enthusiasm to start selling the solution prematurely. Sufficient time should be devoted to understanding in detail the customer's issues.

The objective of the sales call for the first level is usually fairly clear: You want the order. The next level down depends greatly on the situation, but there is a commonality between a sale and any other. Here are some suggestions for level two that are often important:

    a) Sort out the existing installation/service.
    b) Persuade them to come out with a request for proposal (RFP)/tender.
    c) Dispatch all the competitors by nailing down your strengths.
    d) Build up political clout (a relationship) in the sale by getting the votes that count.
    e) Win the technical recommendation of your solution incorporation and place it into the RFP.
    f) Prepare the financial argument (i.e., ROI, payment terms, etc.).

Each process will create a series of sales calls that will together meet your overall objectives.

    Sales-campaign plan's documentation:

    a) Statement of objective
    b) Competitors
    c) I can win if I can persuade him that he really needs . . .

CRITERIA	Your Offering		Competitor 1		Competitor 2	
	Strength	Weakness	Strength	Weakness	Strength	Weakness
SOCIAL						
FINANCIAL						
EMOTIONAL						
POLITICAL						
TECHNOLOGICAL						

09. The Role of Social Media in Sales

The power of social media is it forces necessary change.

—Erik Qualman

For those of us in sales before the year 2000, you will remember there were only F2F (Face to Face) sales. From year 2000 onward, social media really took a hold on a global scale and change the way sales will be conducted forever, in all industries including B2B (Business to Business) sales. Social media has changed the sales cycle in some industries from weeks and days to hours. All businesses are active on the Internet and social media site to create awareness, generate interest, desire, and purchase i.e. AIDA online (Awareness, Interest, Desire, Act).

For the sales manager, it does not really matter if it is F2F sales or a combination of social media as is the case for B2B sales. The principles of salesmanship are still the same. The social website is like the virtual sales manager or calling card and creates the first impression for the customer. This is similar to your first meeting (i.e., the first three minutes in F2F sales) to create a good first impression to the customer. The *content* is key and will require some effort and thinking directed to induce (or motivate) the customer to contact the sales manager. Usually in today's social media sales environment, the customer already has done 60 percent of his research of the buying process as compared to the F2F buying in the past.

Sales managers use the power of social media such as LinkedIn, Facebook, blogs, forums, and Twitter, to identify opportunities, get insights into prospective businesses, earn the first engagements, and develop relationships. There are some difference between F2F only sales and using a combination of social media plus F2F. See table below:

S/No	F2F Sales	Social Media Sales (plus F2F)	**Benefits**
1	You call customer (cold calling)	Customer calls you	**Better Qualification**
2	Cannot start with the right contact person, unaware of needs, budgets, timelines	Engages right people from start and gets all the right information	**Reduce sales cycle time**
3	Limited time to propose solution, cannot cover details	Become trusted advisor	**Cover entire sales cycle and After sales services**
4	Customer resistance and objections	Relationship based on knowledge – better listening on customer's part	**Insight into customer processes**
5	Due to limited sales resources, some opportunities are lost.	Spot opportunities early	**Increase sales leads**

The worst of all selling failures comes when it is time to ask for an order (i.e., when it is time to ask for specific action from the customer). Take an example from the retail industry; people are routinely permitted to wander around in stores, look at merchandise, and leave empty-handed without ever being put through an organized, scripted sales presentation that leads to a "close" or even having their names and contact information captured for follow-ups. The fact is there is no money to be made until somebody sells something. It is my experience that little gets sold without the sales manager directly asking for the order.

A prospect is worthless without conversion. If you are not actively turning your prospects into buyers, then you're missing out on a lot of potential revenue. Therefore, social media is only part of the equation. The sales manager is ultimately accountable for closing the deals and generating revenue.

10. Need Engineering

If you do not know how to ask the right question, you discover nothing.
—W. Edwards Deming

Conventional wisdom says "Sell benefits." In the information age, a more useful tool is the saying "Sell *consequence*." Why? *Consequence* is the relation between an effect and its cause, or put in another way, it means "something that logically or naturally follows from an action or condition." This makes the customer aware that there are consequences to his actions. If he selects not to make a decision, there is one outcome, and if he chooses to make a decision, then there is another outcome. *Consequence* amplifies the customer's pain/problem and makes him want to find a solution prior to knowing what you, a sales manager, have to offer as a solution.

In the current market conditions where sales is for the replacement or retrofitting of products or services that are currently in use, it is imperative that the replacement products or services will improve efficiency, effectiveness, and safety (i.e., value selling). The sales manager needs to make an assessment of the potential customer's business operations and identify what improvements can be achieved by the product or service to be implemented. How can this be done?

Pains/problems are discovered by such questions as the following:

    a) "That must cause you all sorts of problems?"
    b) "Does that mean that . . .?"
    c) "And does that affect . . .?"
    d) "If you had a solution, what would it mean to you?"
    e) "And what else would it mean?"

This is a process-oriented approach to identify and record the customer's pains/problems (i.e., "A systematic series of actions directed to some end"). At the close, the pain/problem you discovered can be used to summarize the need found prior to the close (i.e., after you have discussed your product, it is worth reminding your prospect of the agreed pain/problem before you ask him for the order).

<u>Fig. 2: Process-Oriented Approach</u>

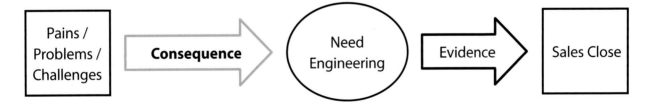

If you ask most sales managers what their plans are to win a particular sale, they will talk in terms of evidence. They are going to give lines like the following:

a) "I am going to show . . ."
b) "We will demonstrate . . ."
c) "At the existing customer site, he will see . . ."

This response is natural, but in my view, it is incorrect. Merely showing evidence begs a big "So what?" from the prospective customer. The sales manager should talk in terms of the needs he wants to create (i.e., "I will persuade him that he needs . . .").

An important part of the need engineering is also to identify and convince what the customer has to do (i.e., "Can you please . . ."). Some examples can be the following:

a) Arrange an appointment to meet the end user.
b) Set a date to meet the consultants to clarify the RFP.
c) Set up a study team to prepare a GAP analysis.
d) Tell them the rules of engagement for the project.
e) Set up start dates for the site survey.
f) Set up training dates before the trial is planned.
g) Set up the method of monitoring the progress of the plan.
h) Order the appropriate equipment four weeks before the installation is planned.

This is important because, ultimately, it is the customer who has to progress through their own organization's due-diligence process of purchasing to the point where an order can be issued. This process has to be in parallel to all the actions of the sales manager. The sales manager cannot be running whilst the customer is dragging his feet. If this is allowed to happen, the outcome will be a prolonged sales cycle. More on how to get a commitment from the customer in the chapter entitled "Sales Call."

11. Stimulating the Customer to Act

A moment's insight is sometimes worth a life's experience.

-—Oliver Wendell Holmes Sr.

In the previous chapter, the emphasis was on asking the right questions. That is a good practice for salesmanship. However, all sales managers are trained to ask questions. From the customer's perspective, after he has met with two or three sales managers asking basically the same questions, he will be fed up. Therefore, the sales manager has to provide *insight* to stimulate the customer's interest and keep the customer engaged.

Aristotle was the Greek philosopher who studied the art of persuasion. Aristotle taught Alexander the Great how to properly argue and give a public speech. In the 4th BCE, Aristotle wrote a book entitled *The Art of Rhetoric*. In this book, Aristotle compiled the three methods of persuasion. He called them ethos, pathos, and logos (Greek). Ethos (or the ethical appeal) means to convince an audience of the author's credibility or character. Pathos (or the emotional appeal) means to persuade an audience by appealing to their emotions. Logos (or the appeal to logic) means to convince an audience by use of logic or reason.

The sales manager would use ethos to show to his customers that he is a credible source and is worth listening to. Ethos is the Greek word for character. Ethos can be created by the sales manager's friendly disposition, choosing the right language that is appropriate for the type of customer, using correct grammar whilst introducing the product and services and keeping an open mind to different and opposing views.

The sales manager would use pathos to invoke sympathy from his customers, to make the customer feel what the sales manager wants them to feel. The sales manager would provoke the customer to instigate action, i.e., why are you working our hours on a plan when the task could be accomplished in one hour by using the new version of the software (upgrade). Pathos is used by the sales manager to prompt action from the customer by using meaningful language, emotional tone, narrating "war stories," past experience, what the customer's competition is doing, and other implication if decision is not made now.

The word logic is derived from "logos." The sales manager uses logos by means of his theoretical or technical knowledge, citing facts (very important), using historical case studies, analogies and by putting forth logical arguments. The foundation for the construction of logical arguments to provoke customers and prompt the desire action is *data*. The sales manager will need the support of other functional teams in his organization to prepare such sales and marketing collateral.

The sales manager cannot directly challenge the customer, especially on the core or direct business processes of the customer's organization. Such a direct challenge to the customer will be foolhardy on the part of the sales manager. There is a good chance that such a sales manager will be barred from customer for good. Our CEO's son was invited to joins us on a sales visit to a shipping company. Once the technical director had introduced himself, our CEO's son started talking about naval architecture and what should be considered for ship stability and strength. The technical director interrupted him and asks: "How many ships have you build"? Our CEO son's obvious answer was none. Than the technical director said that he has been building ships for the last 15 years. That was the end of our sales visit.

A more prudent approach would be to challenge the customer first on the non-core or indirect business processes. That is to review the supporting processes e.g. planning, order processing, delivery, accounting, etc; Once an area has been identified the sales manager will than evaluate the "Effectiveness, Efficiency and in some cases also Safety" level of the processes. This will change the playing field and put the sales manager on the same level as the customer regardless of the advance, industry or domain knowledge, of the customer.

The goal of the sale manager is to close the deal and secure a customer. Oftentimes, the customer is agreeable but just does not make a commitment. The sales manager must be prepared with logical arguments on the cost of delay in decision-making. The sales manager has to provide an insight into what is actually happening. The following short story may be a good example: A man was walking by a farm and notices a farmer hard at work, sawing timber but making little progress. After a while, the man approaches the farmer and suggested that it would be better if the farmer could first "sharpen his saw." Back came the reply immediately: "I have no time for that, I need to saw the timber." The sales manager need to show the customer that there is a cost of not doing and staying with the status quo. What is the cost of error? What is the cost of failure? What are the impact and risk on the business of not doing the decision today?

"The timeline has been shortened to 'Right now'."

12. Target Price vs. Cost Plus

Customers do not see it as their job to ensure the manufacturer a profit. The only sound way to price is start out with what the market is willing to pay.

—Peter F. Drucker

The Western managers' thinking is still based on the cost-plus method of pricing a product or service. This approach is based on calculating the cost of production (i.e., material, labor, and manufacturing) and then putting a margin on top. Therefore, in this pricing mind-set, there is little or no pressure to reduce the production cost of the product or service. The challenge is shifted to sales. Not only must the sales compete with other suppliers but also convince the customers to pay a higher price. This approach may work for consumer products that already have an established brand. It hardly ever works for capital-goods sales.

It was Taiichi Ohno the father of the <u>Toyota Production System</u>, which became <u>Lean Manufacturing</u> in the U.S., who said, "Costs do not exist to be calculated. Costs exist to be reduced." With the emergence of the lean enterprise and global competition, companies face ever-increasing levels of competition. As competition becomes more intense, companies are compelled to learn to become more proactive in the way they manage costs. The first way is to manage the cost of future products. The second is to manage the cost of the existing products, and the third is to harness the entrepreneurial spirit of the workforce.

Target costing coupled with value engineering (VE) lays the foundation for a sustainable competitive advantage for a business entity by managing its costs. Target costing is primarily a technique for profit protection. See the figure below.

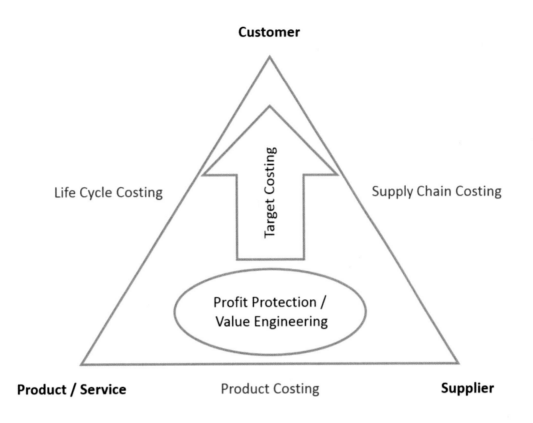

13. Segmentation

"Culture" is a finite segment of the meaningless infinity of the world process, a segment on which human beings confer meaning and significance.

—Max Weber

The sales manager needs to find characteristics of the focus-market segment in relation to the product or service (i.e., research the unique selling proposition [USP]).The development of the USP is critical for winning against competition.

During the segmentation exercise, the sales manager will sort into the priority sequence the list of potential prospects in the market segment. Because of this list, the sales manager is in a position to play the odds. Without this list, the idea of playing the odds will remain just that—an idea.

The list needs to be long enough so that you have a statistical chance of success.

Finally, the sales manager must make a decision, and that is to hit the list hard. The purpose of the list is to progress each item to the point where it can be qualified using a formal checklist, such as that represented by the SALESMAN mnemonic. It is impossible to call on all of them at once. The selection criteria need to be developed to create ABC and Pareto analysis lists to categorize and prioritize the customer database for the sales call/campaign.

The purpose of segmentation is to find the big and easy sales. Likewise, the goal of qualification is to weed out the small and hard ones that slip through the net. But first you must cast the net.

For the segmentation of the prospects list, the sales manager can use two techniques used in material management. One is Pareto analysis. (While it is common to refer to Pareto as the 80/20 rule—which is the assumption that, in all situations, 20 percent of causes determine 80 percent of problems, this ratio is merely a convenient rule of thumb and is not and should not be considered an immutable law of nature). We can theorize using Pareto analysis that 20 percent of the prospects will generate 80 percent of the sales turnover.

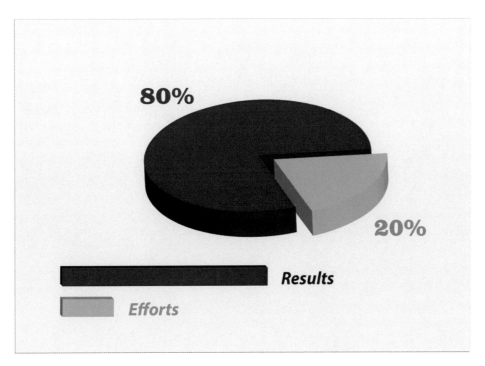

Second is ABC analysis (or selective inventory control) is an inventory-categorization technique. ABC analysis divides an inventory into three categories: A items have very tight control and accurate records, B items have less control compared to A items and good records, and C items have the simplest controls possible and minimal records. The ABC analysis suggests that prospects in the call list are not of equal value. Thus, the prospects are grouped into three categories (A, B, and C) in the order of their estimated importance.

Having categorized and sorted the prospects list into A, B, and C lists, resource planning can be made based on the estimates of time required to call and follow up on each prospect. Past experience has shown that a sale of one million and a sale of one hundred thousand require the same effort and steps in the sales cycle. Therefore, it is pertinent that the sales effort is directed at the A list of prospects.

Segmentation (by market sectors, industry vertical, geography, price, etc.,) is a great tool available for the deployment and direction of the organization's limited sales resources to achieve the set goals within the constraints of the financial period.

14. Qualification

If you don't meet the standards, then you don't qualify.

—Harold Ford Jr.

Most sales managers, if asked what stops them from selling twice what they currently achieve, will reply, "Time—there is just not enough of it."

What is their biggest time waster? No, it is not travel. It is not paperwork or internal meetings. The sales manager's biggest time waster is a sale they lose. If they are winning one in four, then three quarters of their time is wasted. Ask them what they must do about it. They will usually answer "Qualification." So let's look into *qualification* in more detail.

Why do the qualification of leads? The key reason is to use time more effectively. The message is clear: If you know you are going to lose or are very likely to lose, then get off that sale as soon as you can. Don't waste time writing that proposal or preparing that demonstration. Qualification can double your sales.

Qualification is probably the single most important activity when one is selling nonconsumer goods. *Qualification* means "only bidding when you have a good chance of winning." Too many sales managers delude themselves into thinking that they have a chance of winning a sale when the conditions are manifestly against them. They then spend many weeks of work on a small chance—time they could better spend by looking for more opportunities. They end up winning three out of ten when the top sales managers win eight out of ten.

How can this trap be avoided? The following three steps should help immeasurably:

a) At a sales meeting, the sales manager should prepare a formal checklist of questions designed to establish the presence of factors that are likely to make them lose. It should cover competition, decision process, needs for specials, and political influences.
b) Prior to allocating support and resources (i.e., customer visits, entertainment, etc.), it should be mandatory that the situation should be reviewed by management against the checklist.
c) The output from the meeting must be one of these: "Yes, we will bid"; "No, we will not bid because of factors x, y, and z"; or "Yes, we will bid *but* only if the prospect will make the

following commitment [e.g., a) He will relax his insistence on feature X. The consultant will set up a meeting with the CEO. b) The IT department will state in writing that they will give the business to someone other than the current supplier given conditions A, B, and C]."

Qualification is not a simple yes/no process. By far the most common situation is that the result of qualification will be the identification of sales calls. To qualify, look for the problems, not the goods things. To qualify, a checklist is needed, and SALESMAN is a simple memory aid. Most people qualify by looking for the good things in the sale. What they should do is look for the bad things. This pessimism will quickly identify sales activity.

S	A	L	E	S	M	A	N
Scope	Adversity	Landscape	Engagement	Solution	Money	Authority	Need
Size / Scale	Risk / Challenge	Competition / SLEPT Factors	Formal / Structured	USP	Budget / Time	Sponsor / Decision Maker	Efficiency / Effectiveness / Safety

There are two parts to the qualification process (i.e., evaluating and communicating). Test the temperature by evaluating the eight factors and then identify the sales calls necessary. The most important activity is in identifying the sales calls. Unless the qualification results in a list of sales calls, the qualification cannot be considered fully justified.

Experience shows that sometime after being introduced to SALESMAN, salespeople slip into the habit of making a token effort at scoring the sale then stop. When they do this half effort, they are wasting their time.

The real purpose of qualification is to identify sales calls. It does not take long to go through the process. Qualification is an ongoing process. The situation will change as it develops. Walking away from a lousy situation is a positive act. It will release time for more important work. Sales managers should not be scared to challenge these problems with the prospect. "Convince me I should bid" is the attitude.

On the other side, qualification can be a good means of communication by which to draw in the other stakeholders in the organization or supply chain. By getting a buy-in or commitment from these parties early in the sales cycle, it will make it that much easier to get an allocation of support resources for customer visits, demonstrations, etc.; the sales manager will not have to carry the burden all by himself if he gets the involvement of management in pursuing the opportunity.

15. Sales Call

The top salesperson in the organization probably missed more sales than 90% of the sales people on the team, but they also made more calls than the others made.

—Zig Ziglar

A good way to start preparing for a sales call or visit is to ask this question: Why must a customer buy from us? The sales manager will be compelled to think about a differentiator of his solution that separates it from the competition.

For the sales manager, sales calls are the key to achieving success in sales. However, a unique selling proposition (USP) has to be developed and adopted before any sales visit. In order to formulate the USP, the sales manager must understand the market factors and the competition and have a good understanding of the customer. The USP can be that one thing that says "Only me." This is what sets you apart from the rest; this can be a function, a feature, or a benefit of your proposed solution.

Some sales managers find selling far easier than others. If you ask sales managers to tell you what they have to do to make it easier for them, they will usually say "more information" and "independence to act." This degree of freedom is what sales managers would like to call sales authority. Authority is not arrogance and also not parental authority; it is the inbuilt way they have of carrying themselves.

Many factors are important to give an air of authority, such as confidence in self, confidence in product, confidence in company, knowledge, dress, and presence. However, the fundamental difference between the manifestation of authority and the lack of it is that the authoritative sales manager knows exactly what he wants in any situation, but that in itself is not enough. Authority requires three things:

a) Direction: The sales manager knows what he wants in any situation. He has a point of view or a corner to fight.
b) Tenacity: Having a direction is no good if you keep changing it too frequently.
c) Say "No": The ability to say "No." He knows where he is not going and cannot be intimidated. He has the knowledge to back it up and does not display an attitude of "I don't need your business."

Direction is different from *destination*. Wanting the order is not a direction. Every sales manager says that. A direction has to do with the path you follow. A direction has to do with sales-call objectives. If you ask any salesman to state clearly the objective of their next sales call, you will notice that each objective can be restructured to start with the phrase "I want." Ask any sales manager if this is all that *direction* is—knowing clearly what you want. Obviously, it's not; it misses out the prospect. For sales managers, a direction should start with "Can you please . . ." Know what you want the other party to do. This is getting a commitment from the customer.

Other examples are "Can you please set up a joint meeting with your boss" and "Can you please put a date in your diary for a demo." These are the things that drive the sale forward.

To achieve authority, a fundamental step is this; prior to any situation, you should examine the phrase "Can you please . . ." The critical completion of this sentence will determine how you conduct a meeting and/or make it much more direct. This technique insists that call objectives should be black-and-white (i.e., at the end of the call, it can be *clearly* seen if you succeeded). You know you have a clear objective if you can go into the call and say to the prospect: "Can you please . . ." and he can answer with merely a yes or no. The "Can you please . . ." statement should include active verbs such as

a) Sign this MoU

b) Talk to your CEO

c) Write a memo to your operations manager

d) Put a date in your diary for our next meeting

Sign, talk, minute, write, and *put a date in diary for* . . .

It should then, if possible, include a commitment to the prospect. The statement should look like this: "Can you please [active verb] plus [something specific]." There are a number of major advantages:

a) You have a specific statement you can make to the prospect to open the call.

b) You can have a single-minded attitude at the close, and the prospect already knows what you want.

c) You have something very specific to use as a basis for planning the call.

d) You know exactly where you are with the prospect.

e) With practice, you will aim for more ambitious objectives.

f) It is easy to know what you will do in the call and after it. The problem is to determine what your prospect will do.

When consultants and other intermediaries are involved in the decision, absolute realism is essential because they can be very time-consuming and technical. The sales manager should answer this question at the very onset: When consultants are involved, does the record show that your company is more likely to win or less likely to win and by how much?

One suggestion for handling the situations with consultants is to talk them through the flowchart. The flowchart is a very black-and-white view designed to focus the mind. Two points are not self-evident. Will the client check the last three recommendations?

a) Yes, he will, and the consultant spreads his business. This means the consultant is unbiased and not in someone's pocket. You can happily bid.

b) Yes, he will, and the consultant always recommends the same supplier. This means that the consultant is on a commission, or he is recommending what he knows how to install. You should tell the client why you are withdrawing.

c) No, he won't check. You should respect the client's position but tell the client why you cannot take the risk of bidding.

d) The consultant will not be involved in the implementation process? This commitment is a tough one, but it is the only way the client can ensure an unbiased recommendation.

Fig. 4: Consultants / Other Third Parties

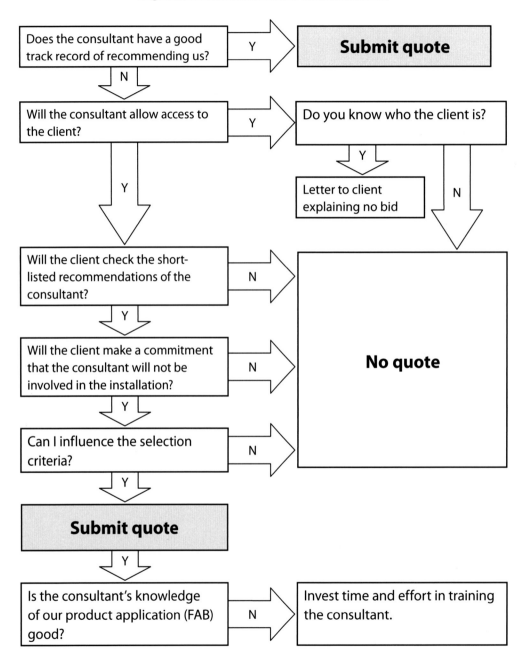

16. Relativism in Sales

> Concentrate your strengths against your competitor's relative weaknesses.
>
> —Paul Gauguin

Relativism is defined in the *Merriam-Webster* dictionary as "the belief that different things are true, right, etc., for different people or at different times."

Blind Men and the Elephant—A Picture of Relativism and Tolerance

The Blind Men and the Elephant is a famous Indian fable that tells the story of six blind sojourners that come across different parts of an elephant in their life journeys. In turn, each blind man creates his own version of reality from that limited experience and perspective. In philosophy departments throughout the world, *The Blind Men and the Elephant* have become the poster of relativism and tolerance of difference in opinion.

Relativism in salesmanship is relevant to the way competition is handled during the sales cycle. This is best illustrated by the following short story: Two sales managers were walking in the wilderness when they heard the roar of a lion. One of the sales managers got scared and said to the other, "We are dead for sure. We can never outrun a lion." The other sales manager smiled and said, "I am not worried. I don't have to outrun the lion as long as I can run faster than you." The moral of the story is you don't need a perfect product or service to be successful. You just have to be better than your next competitor.

It is important that a sales manager has a good grasp of the relativism concept for practical sales application. No two sales cycles are the same; the application is on a case-by-case basis. First, focus on the particular customer and his specific needs. Second, pay attention to the relative strength and weakness of the competitor making the other sales bid for the deal. Since the sales manager does not have direct control or cannot influence the way your customer or competitor behaves, all the sales manager can do is direct his efforts on what he can "do differently to correlate his strength against the relative weakness of the competitors."

Please try and solve this puzzle: How would you make the line A—A¹ shorter without touching the line?

A ━━━━━━━━━━━━━━━ A¹

(The solution is provided in Appendix C, but please try and use the concept of relativism to solve this puzzle.)

17. Beating the Competition

> Winning isn't everything, it's the only thing.
>
> —Vince Lombardi

For the sales manager, the battlefield cry is "I can win *if* . . . [e.g., "I can persuade him that . . .".]." This phrase is a tool to help prepare calls once the objective is decided. It helps to ensure that the battle is fought on your terms while recognizing the need to establish real needs at the prospect's site. It replaces the conventional-wisdom phrases like "What does he really want?" or "Sell him the decision criteria."

It is also a tool to help you in the call as you have a checklist of topics that *must* be discussed. There is little point in moving on unless they are covered; otherwise, you don't win! So you will spend the bulk of your time discussing important customer issues—not your product.

In using this preparation tool, you should appreciate that there are several areas to cover. You must win, if possible, in all of them (i.e., social, legal, emotional, political, and technological). The "I can win if . . ." statements should **not** say "I can win if I can demonstrate X, Y, and Z." They should say "I can win if I can make the customer really need . . ."

CRITERIA	You		Competition	
	Strength	**Weakness**	**Strength**	**Weakness**
SOCIAL				
FINANCIAL				
EMOTIONAL				
POLITICAL				
TECHNOLOGICAL				

The sales manager needs to review the process for beating the competition and work out why the prospect should buy his proposed solution rather than some other generic product. Many sales managers sell *a* system rather than *their (feeling of ownership)* system. This review should change that.

a) For the sale, you must finish the sentence "I can win *if* . . ." with emphasis on the *I*. To help with this exercise, draw the battleground chart and work out where you are different from your competitors' specific feature by specific feature. Add in other angles, such as references in this application area, people with specific skills, specific strengths, financial aspects, etc.

b) Now you can say "I can win *if* I can persuade the CEO that he really needs the functions [specific] of our solution."

c) However, this is essentially a statement about winning technically, and many sales get the technical win but lose politically.

d) At this stage, you should go through the voting-clout exercise described above to establish who the key players are.

e) You can now make a number of statements with a pattern like this: "I can win politically *if* I can persuade Mr. X that he really needs the solution based on "insight" into his operations.

f) Having established these statements, the next step is to convert them into specific calls.

g) Who is calling on whom? (i.e., Map your team to that of the customer's team.)

h) Construct the flowchart diagram on direction and commitment (see example in Appendix B)

It is a usual sales practice to prepare proposals for the prospect. A proposal takes up a lot of time, can represent contractual commitments, and is rarely useful as a selling tool, and the prospect often demands one. The sales manager should not start investing time and effort in preparing an elaborate proposal. This should only be done much later in the sales process after the qualification of the account.

Fig. 5: Proposal—Suggested Handling

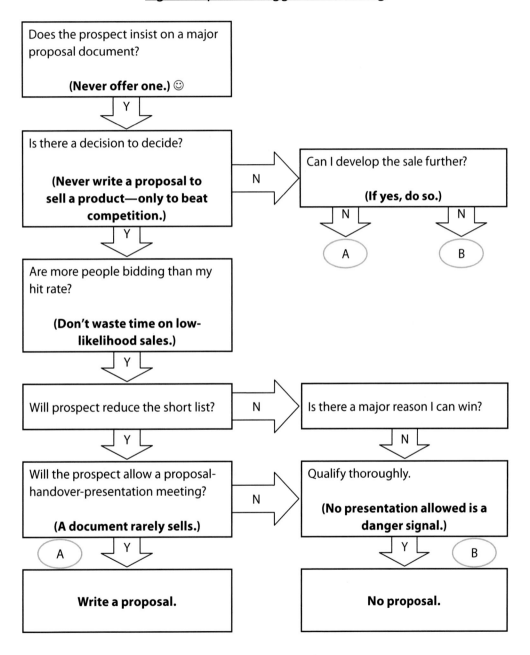

Trials and demonstration accounts should also be discouraged by the sales manager as these rarely make good sales tools for nonconsumer products. Past sales experiences have shown that it is far better to organize reference-site visits at successful customer installations. Also, organizing sessions where the existing happy customer can share his experience with your prospect's evaluation team works far better than any trial or demonstration done by your own technical team.

In the current market conditions, the sales manager can beat the competition by going the extra mile (i.e., by making it easier for the prospect to buy through the consideration of various financial-support options). This can be in the form of a subsidy from the government, a payment term, or a deferred payment. Colin Powell puts it best: "There are no secrets to success. It is the result of preparation, hard work, and learning from failure."

18. Timetable

For centuries, man believed that the sun revolves around the earth.
Centuries later, he still thinks that time moves clockwise.

—Robert Brault

The concept of time is the cornerstone for salesmanship practice. The sales manager needs to comprehend that time past is history; nothing can be done to change the past. Time in the future is uncertain. The only actionable time is the present. Actions in the present will determine the outcome in the future. The sales manager keeps an eye on closing the deal, which should be achieved in the future by taking appropriate actions in the present.

A good way for the sales manager to start thinking about the close is to ask this question: Why must the customer buy now? What is the correlation, if any, to a quarter-close, year-end, budget period, etc.? During a sales cycle's account review, one of the most critical points is when the prospect decides that he does actually have to make a decision (i.e., he has to set up a formal decision process). In a creative sales situation, the sales manager must get this decision to decide fairly quickly, or he will end up wasting time. This event should be his major objective early on in the sales cycle with a statement such as "Can you please agree to make a decision—not necessarily now but in four weeks.

The problem with this last statement is that your objective, as stated, merely gets agreement, which, as we have seen, is inadequate. Somehow we want a physical manifestation of the decision to decide. You might want to rephrase it as follows: "Can you please agree to make a decision." In doing so, we can set a timetable and put dates in diaries plus set up access to key executives and write down your major decision criteria. By establishing a timetable, you get the sale rolling. If you try to establish a timetable and fail, then you will at least be sure that they had little intention of going ahead anyway and you are better off spending your time elsewhere.

Other "decision to decide" objectives might be "Can you please allocate a budget for this project" or "Can you please let me present to your board." The choice depends on the circumstances. The principle is very important.

Example
(Modify to suit your own sales cycle.)

S/No.	Activity	Duration
1	Calls on key Individuals to establish needs	2 days
2	Technical-update seminar	½ day
3	Call to ensure understanding	½ day
4	Customer visit	1 day
5	Demonstration	½ day
6	Day to check the proposal	½ day
7	Presentation of proposal to LOB	1 day
8	Presentation of proposal to the board	½ day
9	Proposal follow-up	1 day

This timetable should, if possible, be agreed with the customer before he formally comes out with a statement of his requirements. After all, you will want to influence the requirements. He has never bought your product before, so you are in a position to tell him how to do it. The advantage of this approach is as follows:

a) You find out if the prospect is serious. Is he "deciding to decide"?
b) He will like to know exactly what it will cost in time
c) You can plan your time and look after other interests.
d) You can ensure access to many levels and a wide range of management by putting it in the timetable.
e) It allows for sales forecasting.
f) You get access to a higher level in case of a never-ending sales cycle.
g) You can mobilize your reference at the right time to get the maximum impact.
h) You can shorten the sales cycle.
i) It can help keep competition out.

19. Giving Evidence

A man with one watch knows what time it is; a man with two is never sure.

—Anonymous

If you ask a sales manager how he is handling a sale, he will usually describe the *evidence* he is giving—that is, he will demonstrate this, show the other, present something else, write a proposal, have a user visit, etc. This is a natural result of the fact that various events are set up to present the *evidence*. However, I believe that sales managers should think of a sales campaign in terms of commitments they want and a contact's agreement to a timetable and to a particular feature/function.

Evidence with no needs created will lead the prospect to say "So what?" Likewise, needs with no evidence will lead the prospect feeling dissatisfied, and you could lose the sale. So you must give thorough evidence at all levels. Each person you call on will want appropriate evidence.

Fig. 6: Venn Diagram of Evidence and Needs

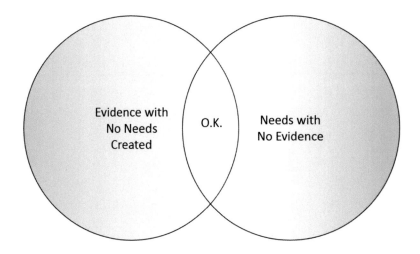

The sales manager should also think in terms of the needs he must create and the commitment he must get for those needs. Only then can he think through the *evidence* and make sure he presents it thoroughly at all levels. Claims should be supported by success stories, reference-site visits, and live demonstrations.

The sales manager should have a call-preparation checklist/worksheet (i.e., calling on company, name of contact person, and designation of the contact). He must also have the statement of direction and commitment (i.e., "Can you please [active verb] . . ."). The sales manager also should think of if statements (e.g., "I can win *if* I can persuade Mr. X that he really needs function Y."

CRITERIA	Your Offer		The Alternative (i.e. Competitor's offer, or "Do Nothing")	
	Strength	**Weakness**	**Strength**	**Weakness**
SOCIAL				
EMOTIONAL				
POLITICAL				
TECHNOLOGICAL				
FINANCIAL				

A demonstration is an important milestone in the sales cycle. If you think of any demonstration that you have seen, you will realize that after the event, you actually remember very little of it—probably just one major event or product feature, if at all.

Your customers watching your demonstration will be exactly the same—they will probably just remember one thing. If they are only going to remember one thing, surely it is fundamental that you choose what they remember. Your whole demonstration should be designed to highlight one main theme. At the end, the customer must say, "Well, if there is one thing that they have got, it is . . ."

Yet most demonstrations present what is essentially a romp through the features. The customer sees fifty features and is left to choose for himself what he remembers; typically, he remembers the mistakes the presenter makes. If your customer is going to remember only one thing and you are going to choose it, then you must choose some major customer benefit. It would be wasteful to highlight just one feature. You must use the features to highlight the major benefit.

You want your customer to walk away saying something like one of the following: "With you, I will give a real customer service" or "With you, my business growth will be really secure" or "With you, my staff will save a lot of time." Once you have selected your theme, which is a risk-taking exercise, every part of the presentation/demo should be related to it—even the talk about your company's history. Give yourself a single bullet and aim between the eyes (i.e., neither bird shot nor aiming in the general direction of the target).

The sales manager is ultimately responsible for the outcome of the demonstration that will probably be conducted by a team of engineers or technical consultants. The demonstrations have to be well prepared as usually there is only once chance during a sales cycle. Start with the following:

a) statement of direction and commitment,
b) selection of the theme necessary (What must be highlighted? What single thing do you want them to remember about your company and product at the end?),
and
c) construction of the demonstration or showmanship (How can I highlight the disadvantage of the old way? What are the advantages of the new approach?). Please make an effort to apply

the "Keep it simple, stupid" (KISS) idea. Finally, orchestrate the close (i.e., How will you arrange to be able to close?).

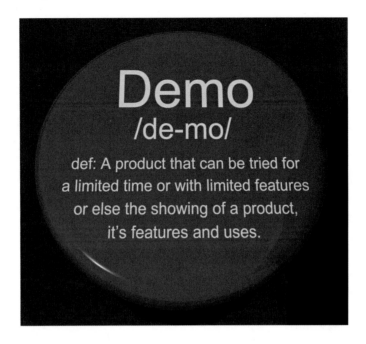

Showmanship appeals are a key part of demonstrations. These are enthusiasm, audience, involvement, comedy, surprise, contrast, conflict, sex appeal, music, color, skill, momentum, grooming, physical action, nothing going on for too long, timing, elimination of extraneous props, people, etc.

It is important that throughout the demonstration, the sales manager and his team maintain a friendly disposition. Let me clarify what I mean by "friendly disposition." This does not mean we say yes to all the work items and sales conditions. There is a way to say no without being arrogant or aggressive. Herbert Bayard Swope put it best: "I cannot give you the formula for success, but I can give you the formula for failure—try to please everybody."

A sales manager needs to be well attired, have a clean haircut, and have on a good pair of clean shoes. This is the package the customer sees even before a word is said. The handshake should be firm, and the sales manager should maintain eye contact with a friendly manner. When the customer is talking, it is wise to respond with an encouraging nod to provide feedback that you are listening to what is being said. Never get yourself in an argument or confrontation with a customer—even if he is wrong. Especially in Asia, you need to give face (i.e., just let it go by first as a sign of respect). You can always come back and clarify the issue at the next opportunity, possibly under different circumstances (e.g., an individual meeting). The same applies for telephone calls, e-mails, and other written forms of communication.

It is recommended that the corporate-profile presentation's deck should be three to five slides that give a precise overview of the company. There is no big advantage to have a lengthy corporate-profile presentation during the solution demonstration. This can be better covered during the proposal stage.

Most importantly, always remember this simple definition of sales: "We help them *buy*." The sales manager must find ways to make it easy for the prospect to make a purchase decision. Thus, the sales manager has to be well prepared for giving evidence on needs for the product, needs for the implementation, needs for the services, etc., by means of referring customer cases as applicable and appropriate.

20. Objective Avoidance

Actual sale action starts after the customer says, No.

—Lothar Beinke

It is highly unusual that on the first sales call, the customer will right away confirm the order. The usual experience is that due to several factors, the first reaction from the customer will be to decline the request for meeting, which is far from him saying yes to a buy decision. Due to the usual operation duties, the customers are too focussed on running the day-to-day business to look for improvements in efficiency, effectiveness, or safety improvement.

Fear, uncertainty, and doubt (FUD) are often the key contributors to the customer's "No" response. Most people have a fear of making a wrong decision, so they would rather not make a decision at all or prefer to take a collective or group decision. The sales manager can offer a trial without obligations, deferred payments, or an extended warranty to ease decision-making.

Uncertainty is related to a future outcome of a decision to purchase. If the sales manager can provide evidence of the current customer base, this will provide support that the company is here to stay. A customer reference will provide assurance to the customer and remove uncertainty in his decision-making process.

Doubt is the presence of the possibility that "what is promised at sale may not be delivered in terms of quantity or quality." The sales manager can remove doubt by inviting the customer for a site visit of the production facility, warehouse, after-sales support center or training facilities.

DOUBT KILLS
MORE DREAMS
THAN FAILURE
EVER WILL.......

There are several types of objections that will be raised by the prospective customer:

S/No.	Objection	Handling
1	**Skepticism**	When the customer expresses, skepticism, *offer proof.*
2	**Indifference**	When the customer expresses indifference, *probe to uncover unrealized needs.*
3	**Misunderstanding**	When the customer's objections are due to a misunderstanding, *probe to confirm the need and make a support statement to clear up the misunderstanding.*
4	**Drawback**	When the customer's objections are due to a drawback, *remind the customer of the benefits already accepted and, if necessary, probe for needs.*

The sales manager's aim should be to solve the customer's problems, but he must not forget to deliver value. This means he has to do more for the customer by going to the root cause, targeting process improvement and quality improvement, and creating a sustainable competitive advantage. Value thinking can be implemented through the process of identifying soft (qualitative) and hard (quantitative) benefits for the customer.

21. Confronting the Prospect

You cannot escape the responsibility of tomorrow by evading it today.
—Abraham Lincoln

Once the sales manager comes to the realization that he is in a never-ending sales cycle, a decision will have to be reached on what should be the appropriate course of action. He can, if able, do this on his own, or he can call for a meeting of the stakeholders and come to a consensus on the next course of action and the time line with them.

These are some of the scenarios when the sales manager has to set up and confront the problem account and call for a decision. Once the prospect starts to equate the capabilities of all the competitors, the prospect will try to reduce his decision to a few major areas (e.g., "I like their support offering, but your delivery is a lot faster"). In doing this, he will equate various capabilities (e.g., "Both of you have reliable solutions"). He will try to reduce your battleground. If, in fact, your products/services are more reliable than your competitors, you will need to be in there and remind him that

a) he does really need the most reliable solution based on technology as a need and
b) you are more reliable and can prove it. You must fight for your advantages.

When the customer oftentimes gives you assurances of their understanding and support for your proposal, these assurances can cause you to relax your efforts. But they may be his method of keeping your sales activity to a minimum. When the customer keeps moving the goalpost and it becomes apparent to the sales manager that the sales-cycle milestones and time line keep shifting, the sales manager is kept busy with requests for more data and case studies, but they are all for nothing.

When, at times, you may feel that continuous contact during the decision phase will upset the prospect, he will consider that you are pestering him. Good access during the sales cycle is critical to closing the deal. The prospect should be interested and eager to get an update and not seeing your visit as pushy or pestering.

Coupled with the above scenarios and if the sales manager feels that the risk of losing the deal is high, these are some of the options available to the sales manager:

a) Delay the deal for a valid reason (new product).
b) Reset the terms of reference so that all other bids have to reevaluated.
c) Call in a very high-up personality (i.e., a CEO).
d) Restart the deal all over again with another sponsor in the driver's seat.
e) If all else fails, try and get the recommenders discredited (and removed J).

It is generally conceded that one of the major reasons that sales are lost is that the sales manager did not call high enough or wide enough. If calling high is so important, why do so many sales managers fail to call high? There are, I believe, three reasons:

a) They cannot think of a good reason to call.
b) They cannot think of a suitable mechanism to set up the meeting.
c) They are scared of upsetting their current contacts at lower levels.

The following are propositions for each of the questions. They cannot think of a good reason to call? The answer to this problem is the direction and commitment statement. One of the following can be selected:

a) "Can you please set up a date when we will present X to the board,"
b) "Can you please meet X, who is an expert in Y,"
c) "Can you please bring X to a demonstration on Y,"
d) "Can you please agree to give us a fair hearing if we put in the work," or
e) "Can you please specify clearly the business requirements."

By selecting any such statement, the call will have a clear purpose, and there should be little difficulty in handling it. Many people fail to call high because they feel that the only objective is to meet the executive, but their instincts will tell them that such an objective is inadequate. They then fail to select another objective. Once the sales manager makes a decision on the BO planning, the call to the C level is far easier.

They cannot think of a suitable mechanism to set up the meeting? Often a meeting is not set up because the sales manager has been told, at least by implication and sometimes explicitly, that he should not go higher. How can he deal with this situation? There are many ways:

a) Ask you current contact if he minds you contacting higher;

b) Persuade your contact to set up a joint meeting (e.g., "I am unwilling to bid without meeting decision makers");

c) Invite the executive to a nonthreatening seminar or demonstration in conjunction with other prospects or other executives from his company;

d) Have a manager or other superior in your company ring him and set up the meeting. Square it with your contact through, for example, "My sales director has decided to ring your MD. Can you and I get together to decide exactly how to brief them?"; and

e) When you make a sale and the order is being signed, ask that there can be a high-level meeting at least once a year. From then on, access is easy at least once a year. But make sure that such a call is made each year, or the benefit will be lost.

They are scared of upsetting their current contacts at lower levels? Sometimes you will upset your contact by going over his head. You should have a plan in mind to pacify him:

a) When you meet anyone, imply that you believe that it is your right to call on anyone in the organization. Preempt the upset by setting your authority correctly (e.g., "I am sure I could persuade your MD to accept this idea").

b) If he really is upset, set up a meeting to discuss his upset explicitly, but don't be too apologetic (your authority is your precious jewel) even if you agree to avoid future contact. If necessary, take your manager in (e.g., "I hear that we've upset you . . ."). The sales manager should always remember that if he does not meet the C level, he will probably lose the deal anyway.

22. Top Down vs. Bottom Up

Strategy should be developed from the bottom up, not top down . . . . In military
warfare, the serious student of strategy begins with the study of the bayonet.

—*Marketing Warfare*, Ries and Trout

So what should salespeople do? Which approach is preferred, top down or bottom up? Salespeople are often compelled by management to start at the top of the customer's organization. This is expected so the sales manager can find a contact of the C level to start the sales lobby. This will often result in the executive-level management of the customer's organization feeling neglected. Also, the current management school of thought is that most C level would prefer to involve the executive level in the decision-making process.

Past sales experiences provide guidance for the sales manager to start at the bottom and take a bottom-up approach to the sales lobby even if the sales manager already has good connections at the C level of the customer's organization. This is a reflection of the sales manager's genuine attempt to understand and solve the customer's problem. It is like building a house. You need a strong foundation at the bottom to hold and keep in place the structure of the house for now and in the future.

Starting at the bottom gives the sales manager a good opportunity to study and understand the business processes of the organization—its challenges and inefficiencies. Having a good foundation at the bottom will lead to a better understanding of the C-level desires and directions of the organization. It is not necessary that all that the C level says is correct all the time. Some C-level members are far removed from the day-to-day operations and do not completely appreciate the challenges and conflicts faced by the executive level of the organization.

Even if there is no choice but to start at the top, the sales manager should insist that he has a chance to interact with the executive level before prematurely putting up a proposal. This will ensure that the proposal is seen as developed in collaboration with the executive level and therefore is co-owned. There will then be a greater probability of success for the acceptance or implementation of the proposal. By doing so, the sales manager avoids being caught in between the C and executive levels of the customer's organization. The power base can be identified early in the sales cycle. The sales task becomes easier when the executive level presents the proposal as its own to the C level.

Past experiences have shown that when the sales pitch is directed at revenue increase (i.e., effectiveness of the customer's business), it is usually easier to get a buy-in from the C level, and if the sales pitch is directed at cost reduction (i.e., efficiency), it is usually easier to work with the executive level to identify and structure the proposal.

Then the only question remaining is this: when should the sales manager involve his own C level? The usual industry practice has been that the sales manager's CEO will get involved in the sales cycle only at the end—when the deal is about to be signed. The sales manager will do all the groundwork, and once the customer is ready to do the deal, the sales manager's CEO will show up to shake hands and provide the assurance of support to the customer.

In this current time of intense market competition, it is recommended that the sales manager's CEO is involved right from the early stages of the sales cycle to assure the customer that the company is fully supporting the sales manager and is committed to provide quality products and services.

23. Leadership in Sales

> Leadership is a combination of strategy and character. If you
> must be without one, be without the strategy.
> —General H. Norman Schwarzkopf

The sales manager needs to display leadership qualities. In an organization, there will be a conflict of objectives. The desire to close deals and get new customers under intense competition may not be shared by other functional departments (e.g., technical support, software development, and finance). In such a situation, the sales manager must persevere, acknowledging the concerns of the support departments but not relenting. For this to happen, the sales manager needs two important leadership traits: strategy and character.

The sales manager needs the mind of a strategist. The sales manager needs to be able to work with multiple customers (both internal and external with opposing demands) whilst managing his own priorities. The sales manager needs to master the discipline of "starting with the end in mind" (i.e., thinking about what needs to be done before going ahead with it). Essentially, *planning* is the competency to develop sales plans, identify potential customers, plan account strategies, and manage daily, weekly, monthly, and quarterly priorities and objectives. Rick Page puts it best: "Hope is not a strategy."

The sales manager's motivation and drive must be guided by principles (i.e., he is an officer and a gentleman). *Character* is different from *personality*. Some salespeople are very pleasant; however, facing the risk of losing a deal they may have worked on for a long time sometimes makes them compromise their principles. Personality can be rehearsed and displayed in a sales call. However, character is deeper and has to be developed over time by training oneself through the exercise of self-reflection, having self-control, and having respect for all. Abraham Lincoln put it best: "Nearly all men can stand adversity, but if you want to test a man's character, give him power."

"
LEADERSHIP
is the **CAPACITY**
to **TRANSLATE**
VISION into
REALITY
"

The sales manager in pursuit of success in a competitive playing field absolutely needs strategy as a prerequisite. However, the strategy needs to be guided by the sales manager's character. This will prevent the sales manager from inventing con schemes and misleading prospects. Character will guide the sales manager's thinking on delivery in full and on time (DIFOT), quality, and customer satisfaction in return for the financial rewards that result from the sale. The sales manager will be obliged to keep the customer informed and protected whilst operating within his own company policies and observing the industry regulations and the prevailing country laws.

24. Relentless in Sales

A man learns little from victory; much from defeat.

—Chinese Proverb

There are often times during a sales manager's career when success is slow in coming. When I started in the sale of maritime-cargo solutions, it took one year before I was finally able to close my first deal. During this first year, there were times, especially during the time I lost a deal that I worked on for months, I felt frustrated and demoralized and even thought about changing jobs. I am happy that I persevered to finally achieve success. It is really the magic word for salesmanship to work. Giving up is simply not an option.

The life of a sales manager is controlled by his thoughts. His thoughts are driven by his goals. The only way he will achieve his goals is by thinking about the numbers all the time. The sales manager must set his goals (e.g., quarterly targets, bi-annual targets, and annual-revenue targets). He has to convert the financial-revenue goals of the company and break down the numbers to products and services that he can forecast to sell in the calendar year. Most sales managers do not like to go through such an exercise. The most common complaint is we do not yet have a sales pipeline. Nevertheless, the sales manager must do a forecast (i.e., his plan to achieve the revenue goals).

There are some sales managers who keep talking about matters other than selling the product or service during a sales call. This social approach to sales calls is unproductive and wastes so much time. The sales manager must have a purpose and have a clear end goal. The subgoals (milestones) need to be closed in stages in order to arrive at the main goal.

The sales manager has to be proud of his profession. He is an important contributor to the company in particular and the economy in general. Why? Because nothing will happen until the sales manager sells something. Then the whole machinery of the organization is put into gear in order to deliver the product or service to the customer. This, in turn, triggers the supply-chain activities across other entities and support sectors (e.g., shipping and transportation). It is perfectly OK to ask for the order after having completed the various stages of the sales cycle or to make an invite to potential customers to an event or networking session while indicating clearly that the objective is a sale. Why should there be any hesitation?

During my early years in sales, while I was selling ERP systems, I always tested the customer if he was keen to purchase our system by making an offer for paid training even before they had purchased the system. I offered them a trial period and a price tag for the training with the agreement that they will get a credit note for the same amount once they purchased the system. There were some of my colleagues who raised objections to this approach, saying that it is not the industry practice and no one would pay for training. My response to them was this question: "If I cannot sell a few thousand dollars' worth of services to the customer, how can I sell a few hundred thousand dollars' worth of products and services?" You must believe that you are doing your customer a good service by selling them a solution that will help their business in terms of efficiency and effectiveness.

In salesmanship, it is not only the end result that counts; the journey in getting to the end goal is equally important and often times reflect the sales manager's creativity to think outside the box. The sales manager has to find new ways of positioning the product/service to the target prospect. The sales manager must not procrastinate in starting to launch a sales campaign because the solution is only 80 percent of what the prospect needs or the sales manager does not have enough technical knowledge to make a sales call. In my previous company, we attended a sales training. We were divided into four groups and had to compete in several outdoor games with time limits. The consistent outcome was that the group that spent much time on planning how to do something, a lot of talk, arguing, etc., lost to the groups that were willing to quickly jump into action and experiment with what could work for them.

In sales, being relentless translates into an obsession to learn what works and a single-minded, directed effort to pursue sales in the face of rejection and failure. In order to have such a relentless drive, the sales manager must believe in himself, his company (colleagues and team), and his products/services. The sales manager remains polite and professional in his pursuit for the deal, being careful not to be annoying or pushy.

No two deals are the same in terms of sales cycle or closing. The sales manager needs to work with a system to keep him on track. I have personally found Steven Covey's *7 Habits of Highly Effective People* to work great for me. The real value is not in reading the book but in putting into practice the principles. The practice has to be exercised daily, weekly, monthly, and quarterly to ensure the follow-up of the action planned and achieve the set goal. Writing down your action plans and goals is a great exercise that sets the mind into thinking gear and helps it focus on what needs to be done and when.

The first things I do when I wake up are stretch, go to the window, and say aloud, "Today will be a great day. I am happy. I am the best sales manager. I will follow up on a, b, and c, and I will close x, y, and z today." In order to do these in the morning, before I go to sleep, I review my schedule for the next day. I follow this routine religiously—even on the weekends. This helps me during the day to stay focused on my goals.

It is important for the sales manager to celebrate any deal closing; smallness or bigness does not matter. One good way is to keep a bell or gong in the office's pantry area. Once a deal is closed, beat the gong to announce the sale. Invite the team to have a glass of wine or beer. This is very motivating both for the sales manager and the team. Everybody looks forward to such events, making each sale a positive signal for the entire team.

25. Numbers Are the Language of Sales

It's clearly a budget. It's got a lot of numbers in it.

—George W. Bush

We use the word *accounting* far too narrowly in business. Giving an account of a particular case should mean more than describing it financially. It should provide a well-reasoned, explanatory account of what happened and why. Every decision leaves a trace. Making visible the traces of everyone's behaviors helps the organization to see itself (with the benefit of hindsight) from an integrated perspective, to interpret what is happening, to connect the causes with the effects, and to learn from the collective experience of all. It closes the feedback loop. Not only does it facilitate collective learning, but it also, by helping everyone see the impacts of their actions, enriches the workplace and gives everyone a highly motivating sense of their own contribution to the total results.

The sales manager must familiarize himself with the financial concepts of ROI (return on investment), NPV (net present value), IRR (internal rate of return), and PP (payback period). These are important as the customer, after making a financial investment, expects a financial return directly or indirectly as efficiency, effectiveness, and safety are improved. It is not possible to cover NPV, IRR, and PP in technical detail here. Nevertheless, a brief nontechnical explanation is mandatory to provide the reader with an overview.

In finance, *NPV* is defined as "the sum of the present values of incoming and outgoing cash flows over a period of time." This essentially means that time has an impact on the value of a cash flow.

IRR (also referred to as *economic rate of return*) is the rate of return used in capital budgeting to measure and compare the profitabilities of investments. IRR calculations are commonly used to evaluate the desirability of an investment or project. The higher a project's IRR, the more desirable it is to undertake the project. Assuming all projects require the same amount of up-front investment, the project with the highest IRR would be considered the best and undertaken first. Because the IRR is a rate quantity, it is an indicator of the efficiency, quality, or yield of an investment. This is in contrast with the NPV, which is an indicator of the value or magnitude of an investment.

Payback period in capital budgeting refers to the period of time required to recoup the funds expended on an investment or to reach the break-even point. The term is also widely used in other types of investment areas, often with respect to energy-efficiency technologies, maintenance, upgrades, or other changes. The payback period is considered a method of analysis with serious limitations and qualifications for its use because it does not account for the time value of money, risk, financing, or other important considerations, such as the opportunity cost.

26. Problem-Solver Mind-Set

> The heart of all problems, whether economic, political or social, is a human heart.
> —Charles Edwards

The principal argument of the salesmanship school of thought is that profit is a return on knowledge and therefore decision-making has to be modelled on scientific problem solving. For example, a problem has arisen that cannot be solved with existing knowledge. A dogmatic solution to such a situation would be to ignore it or deny it. The scientific response is to explore it, approach it from a different angle, and try and resolve it. In sales, the skills of asking different questions, addressing different agendas, and posing different challenges are rare but urgent. Even the smallest shift in the definition of a problem (or an opportunity) can open up new options.

It was my buddy Ronald Leng, in the year 2001, who introduced me to the "five wives and one husband." This is a very powerful industrial-engineering questioning technique that involves *why*, *what*, *where*, *when*, *who*, and *how*. This questioning technique provides the sales manager with a means to inquire and document in a structured manner complex, unstructured business issues. This technique is process-oriented and improves communication—especially when the information gathered during the sales visit has to be shared with the back-end technical team. Ever since I learned it, I have strongly believed that the adoption of this technique is a prerequisite for the practice of salesmanship.

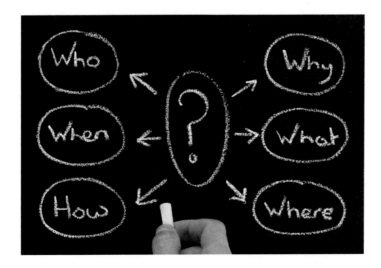

The sales manager with a problem-solving mind-set has a positive attitude in life as well. He does not see a problem; he sees an opportunity. All the advances we made in the world—all that we have achieved—were the results of problem solving. In business, some problems are known, and the customer will acknowledge a proactive search for a solution. Then there are also unknown business problems that the customer may not have identified as of yet. The customer's ignorance can be the sales manager's opportunity. However, efforts to create awareness may meet with a pushback from the customer's team. After finding and stimulating the need (i.e., need engineering), the sales manager can participate in the preference building, shaping of the issues, and structuring of the solution and entrench himself to secure the deal even if there has to be an open-tender bidding.

The sales manager as a solution architect needs to be able to learn from the current customer's processes and initiatives and develop the competency to know what will be applicable and workable for the potential customer. To reach this stage, the sales manager needs to have a deeper understanding of the potential customer's processes and business environment. It is no longer sufficient to sell features and benefits (FAB). The shift is toward identifying the problems, pains, and needs of the potential customer. Having identified the needs, the sales manager then makes a solution proposal to address those needs. So it is no longer about the sales pitch but more about organizing the presentations/demonstrations that are applicable for the particular customer. Each meeting or contact with the customer drives the relationship into a deeper collaboration.

For the sales manager to solve the problem at hand, he has to deliver value to the customer. The value can be in terms of efficiency, effectiveness, or safety improvement.

27. Action Learning in Sales

> The learning and knowledge that we have is at the most but little
> compared with that of which we are ignorant.
>
> —Plato

Companies are rarely brought down by external forces. The majority of corporate crises, sometimes called stall points (when revenue growth slackens dramatically or even reverses), are self-inflicted. The two root causes of stall points are myopia and complacency. *Myopia* is the failure to recognize market shifts until it is too late to respond effectively. *Complacency* is the belief that the company's strategy is invincible.

Marketing myopia can be overcome by the sales manager's ability to be an effective planner or consultant in the industry. This depends on his passion to learn and continuously improve his knowledge in the field and expand his scope in the practice. The sales manager can identify what are the product/ service weaknesses and strengths in the industry. He can acquire knowledge by means of reading or attending seminars or through networking with others in the industry.

Machines become obsolete. Humans can change and adapt through learning. Everything we do involves action, and in a process, there is an opportunity to learn. The aim in action learning is not just to understand the action but to improve it. Therefore, take some time to examine certain actions where you know problems occur, gather relevant data, and talk it over with a colleague or someone with domain knowledge. As a result, try out a new approach, and see what results you get.

Strategy comes in the form of a plan, ploy, pattern, position, or perspective. There is an abundance of literature on strategy; therefore, I will not elaborate on this. What is important in salesmanship is that strategies *emerge*. This can be the outcomes of the sales manager's spontaneous and improvised actions. Complacency can creep in when a sales manager remains nonchalant to the feedback given to him by the prospect and continues to follow religiously the preselected path.

Action learning is a practical and proven means to help salespeople apply learning to important organizational problems. Action learning is also an approach to the everyday work of an individual, a team, or an organization that results in both performance and learning. In the context of management development, action learning provides an opportunity for implementing a continuous-improvement culture and organizational learning that can result in positive and lasting change.

Action learning is a process that involves a small group working on real business problems in real time, taking actions and learning while doing so. There is an abundance of literature on this topic on the Internet. What is important to emphasize here for salesmanship is that the sales manager can harness action learning by means of the PDCA (plan, do, check, and act) cycle.

28. Entrepreneurship in Sales

> Entrepreneurship is neither a science nor an art. It is a practice.
>
> —Peter F. Drucker

Not everyone can be an entrepreneur, and entrepreneurship is not for everyone. Entrepreneurship is the activity of setting up a business or businesses, taking on financial risks in the hope of a profit (www.businessdictionary.com).

Successful salespeople tend to exhibit the trait of entrepreneurship in their dealings with their customers, replacing rigid sales policies on pricing, payment terms, delivery terms, etc., with well-thought-out alternative proposals that create win-win deals and make it easy for the customers to purchase the products or services.

Rather than hiding behind such excuses as "The market is weak," "The customer has no budget," The customer is price-sensitive and cannot afford our product," etc., salespeople with an entrepreneur's flair will always find a solution that is good for both parties.

The entrepreneurship flair of a sales manager has to be coupled with a strong desire to be committed—that is, he has to see through the deal from order to delivery to the collection of the payment. It serves no purpose to put together a creative deal that results either in the customer being frustrated or the company losing money.

There are some very clever salespeople with the entrepreneurship trait that do well for a short period of time and then move on to another company. This is also a lack of commitment on the part of a sales manager notwithstanding the fact that headhunters may be constantly trying make placements with offers of better pay packages.

In the information age, there is a shift from making new sales to having replacement sales. The new sales are dwindling as we move into the future; replacement sales are the growing trend. In order to replace products or services that are currently in place, the sales can only be made based on efficiency and effectiveness. But in order to articulate on efficiency and effectiveness, the sales manager has to be a person that has been committed to his product or service.

Also in the information age, the sales manager's role has been broadening to include product innovation, which is driven by customers. The sales manager can only handle the new responsibilities if he has commitment to the company and the customers. Commitment requires a discipline to focus ones efforts on continuous improvement.

Commitment is also the basis for the sales manager's integration into the customer's organization. In order to get a customer and keep a customer, the sales manager needs to gain an understanding of customer's customer business processes (e.g. supply chain).

Robert Gaertner, CEO of a German MNC Group, puts it best: "Salesmanship in the information age is the coupling of entrepreneurship mind-set and the 'will' to be committed to achieve the company goal."

29. Positive Mental Attitude in Sales

As he thinketh in his heart, so is he.

—Proverbs 23:7

In the real world, an organization will never work well all the time. The sales manager needs to maintain a calm disposition despite things not working out as expected at times. The sales manager needs to take a long-term view of the business and needs a mind-set of continuous improvement. Failing to have these will make him/her become frustrated and may lead to a conflict that leads to the sales manager leaving the organization.

Once I was running a rather-young and small company in the marine industry, and we hired a senior sales manager with several years of sales experience. This person was complaining on a daily basis from the very beginning about the shortcomings of the organization, people, and processes. The backlash was that the team soon started to isolate the manager, which resulted in further complications.

Positive mental attitude (PMA) in sales is essential for the practice of salesmanship. The sales manager with PMA will always start with trying to improve himself as opposed to putting the blame on colleagues, customers, the market, etc. The sales manager with PMA will say "If I am OK, the world is OK." The sales manager with PMA will enjoy the close of a deal and will not cry about one he lost. With PMA, he will learn what went wrong and what needs to be done in the future. The sales manager with PMA will not dwell for too long on negative comments about himself, the product, or the company, marching always forward with a renewed drive each day through being self-motivated to achieve success.

The sales manager with PMA will be a happy person on the inside. This will reflect on his face as cheerfulness despite the weather outside. The glass is always half-full, never half-empty.

The sales manager with PMA will set goals. He will start with the end in mind. He will be aware of the expectations of him, and he will steer toward the goals. In salesmanship, the goal setting is another essential practice that the sales manager must exercise on a daily basis. Goals have to be SMARTER (i.e., specific, measurable, attainable, realistic, timely, evaluate, and reevaluate). The sales manager with PMA will always carry a planner. In the planner, he will note his appointments, his plans, his goals, etc., and refer to these notes on a daily basis.

The sales manager with PMA will be able to use the marketing concept of AIDA (i.e., aware, interest, desire, and action), which is relevant to the sales process, and the product concept of the 7 Ps (i.e., product, price, promotion, place, packaging, people, and process), which is relevant to the sales manager's strategy development for winning an account.

30. Adversity Quotient (AQ)

> In times of great stress or adversity, it's always best to keep busy, to
> plow your anger and your energy into something positive.
>
> —Lee Iacocca

In sales, one will never be spared from stress and adversity. Adversity quotient (AQ) is the measure of how one responds to an adversity (e.g., a challenge, rejection, or unexpected outcome). This is a measure of one's optimism (i.e., mental attitude or worldview). In salesmanship practice, AQ is a critical success factor—even more than EQ (which refers to the ability to recognize one's own and other people's emotions) and IQ (which refers to the measure of human intelligence). In sales, the outcome is ultimately in the hands of the customer. The sales manager can work smart and hard, preparing and delivering the quotation/offer that meets all the customer's needs. Nevertheless, there are many factors that influence the sales outcome, chief among them is the customer.

Actually, this subject was not planned to be included in the original manuscript of *Salesmanship*. However, as I was evaluating a publishing vendor, after I had short-listed the publisher, I postponed my sign-up three times in three weeks. At the third time (on a Friday) when I postponed and raised the issue of proximity (i.e., the publisher was located in another country), the sales representative lost his cool and adopted an aggressive tone and accused me of delaying my decision and "moving the goalpost." Then he wrote me an e-mail that was titled "Let me know for real?" The e-mail read that he was "OK to accept a no!" But that I should decide by next Monday.

Despite the fact that I had already sent many buy signals to this sales representative, he displayed his impatience. In salesmanship school, anger and frustration are emotions that are not to be displayed by a sales manager to a customer whatever the case might be. These emotions are negative energies and will lead to a disruption in the sales cycle and relationship building. Such negative energies will create doubt and raise questions about the professionalism of the service delivery after the purchase. If the customer-facing representative cannot manage his emotions, what about the technical and delivery personnel? Is it the culture of the company to treat customers with an impatient and inappropriate manner?

A customer is free to make a decision for or against the sale. Pushing the customer in an untactful way is only helping the competition. Nudging the customer forward is a skill that the sales manager has to sharpen over a long time. This is not a skill one can acquire by reading a book or simply trying to get lucky. It is best to be patient and avoid a disruption in the sales cycle or relationship building. Once damage is caused, the repair will usually not work, as we have learned from past experiences.

Pushing a customer to make a decision and saying "I will accept your no decision" rather than a postponement is simply being stupid. In salesmanship practice, the no decision is always there by default. The customer does not have to make a no decision for the sales manager. On the contrary, the sales manager wants a yes decision and should rather defer the decision until a yes can be forthcoming. Nudging the customer patiently to a yes decision will require a lot of *thinking* on the part of the sales manager.

It is a pity to see a sale that is so near to a close lost due to the negative actions of the sales manager that were fuelled by anger and frustration. This shortcoming is usually due to a lack of training on the handling of stress and adversity in the sales cycle.

31. Conversations in Sales

Seek first to understand, then to be understood.

—Steven Covey

Cicero was the first major writer to lay down the principles or skills required for a good conversation: speak clearly, speak naturally and not for too long, notice when others want to speak, talk in turns, do not interrupt, be polite, deal conscientiously with serious matters and lightly with frivolous ones, do not speak ill of anyone behind their back, keep to topics of general interest, refrain from talking about yourself, and never lose your temper. Later generations added more rules: remember the other person's name, be an attentive listener, and avoid giving the conversation a purpose outside itself or over and above the pleasure of partaking in it.

Talking too much, too loud, or too long and cutting others off are seen as bad behaviors and rude in general, and the sales manager must avoid such behaviors at all costs. Exercising some form of humility when interacting with others during the sales process can work wonders for the sales manager. It is the principle of "Talking less is more." Salespeople, being enthusiastic to close deals, tend to get carried away and may not know when to pause. They talk themselves into trouble. The same applies during a sales call or product demonstration. Salespeople who talk too much or are too loud will be avoided by the prospects.

In salesmanship, all conversations are interactions with other human beings. The sales manager will show respect to all human beings regardless of their financial standing, position in the organization, race, religion, etc.; the sales manager needs to work with all levels of people and will do so cheerfully. The sales manager will not try to enforce his will on the people below him and suck up to the higher levels. The sales manager will not display arrogance or aggression whether in a sales meeting or a casual chat with friends at a Starbucks.

For the sales manager, conversations are the main mediums of interaction with prospects and customers. During such interactions, the sales manager has an opportunity through conversations, which must be carried out with the right conduct, to endear himself to the prospect or customer. The sales manager, in his role as a consultant, can especially harness conversation skills to share product knowledge without being overbearing. In transactional analysis (TA), there are three types of conversation (i.e., adult-to-adult [professional], adult-to-child [instructional], and child-to-child [conflict]). The sales manager should make a conscious effort to stay at the adult-to-adult conversation (i.e., the professional level).

The goal of conversation in salesmanship is learning (i.e., *deutero-learning*, which is learning from the experiences of others to drive a sale forward).

32. DIFOT (Delivery in Full on Time)

All we are doing is looking at the time line from the moment the customer gives us an order to the point when we collect the cash. And we reduce that time line by removing non-value-added wastes.
—Taiichi Ohno

DIFOT is actually project management from a sales perspective. Even though the sales manager is not directly responsible for the delivery of the products/services, it is in his interest to ensure that delivery takes place as planned so that the revenue can be recognized after the proof of delivery.

The sales manager makes a promise during a sale's close. The operations team has to keep that promise (i.e., DIFOT). In today's competitive marketplace, *DIFOT* means that the product has to be delivered in the right quality, at the right time, at the right price, and at the right quantity. The key word is *right* (i.e., what is right for the customer and the market). If the company delivers a product or service above the right quality, it could be that the cost of production cannot be covered by the selling price. On the other hand, if the company delivers a product or service below the right quality, it is likely to fail, resulting in frequent service calls that result in customer dissatisfaction.

To ensure that the deliver process will run smoothly to satisfy the customer's needs, the sales manager has to be mindful during the "make a promise" portion of the customer stage. The sales manager must have an agreement with the internal customers (i.e., delivery team) that what is promised can actually be delivered. Usually, internal selling is much tougher than selling to external customers. If the sales manager is not sensitive, the result is an internal conflict spiraling to unhappiness in the organization. Politics will start to creep in as each functional team tries to protect its turf. The long-term outcomes of such friction between teams are that the organization becomes uncompetitive and loses market share.

In salesmanship, the sales manager, through conversations, has to convince the supporting teams that the customer is king. The goal of the organization is to satisfy the customer's need. Regardless of the commercial terms (including the selling price), the delivery team should work toward the goal of DIFOT each time and every time. The wisdom in this approach is to ensure the survival of the company during the current intense, competitive market conditions.

The big challenge for the sales manager is to create a win-win mind-set between the internal customers and external customers.

33. Sales Measures

What gets measured gets managed.

—Peter F. Drucker

In most nonconsumer-goods or nonconsumer-services sales, some sales managers are consistently able to sell more than their colleagues. In which area of selling are they better than their colleagues? It is always possible to create a structure as follows: If a sales manager is interested in sales/year, then we can write sales value/year = (sales value/win*wins/year). You can go for one big sale or lots of small ones. This theme can be expanded. The usual format is along the lines of the succeeding formula:

$$\text{sales/year} = (\text{sales/contracts}*\text{contracts/quotes}*\text{quotes/approaches}*\text{approaches/year})$$

To increase sales, one or more of these ratios must be increased. There is no other option, and they can be increased as the performance of the best salesman proves. The question is this: Which ones are the easiest to increase?

Ratio	Impact	Explanation	Factors to Improve
Sales Value/ Contracts	Size of Value	Establish prospecting discipline to search for higher sales. Refuse to bid small ones but keep prospecting.	a) *Listing Priority Prospects* b) *Expanding the Sale* c) *Qualifying out Small Deals*
Contracts/ Quotes	Qualification	Only bid when you know you can win. Firmly get out of losing situations. Know how to sell and build political clout.	a) *Salesmanship* b) *Qualification* c) *Calling High*
Quotes/ Approaches	Segmentation	Establish prospecting disciplines whereby your product can be sold creatively. Call on people who are likely to be interested, not just anyone.	a) *Segmentation* b) *Needs Survey* c) *Referral*

Approaches/ Year	Prospecting	By qualifying out losing situations, you get more time to prospect. The ability to do this implies a faith in prospecting skills. You know that you can walk away from your only opportunity because there is a better one round the corner.	a) *Energy* b) *Enthusiasm* c) *Planning*

34 Data: Intelligence of Business

> In the business world, everyone is paid in two coins: cash and experience.
> Take the experience first; the cash will come later.
>
> —Harold Geneen

In the information age, big-volume applications are critical to the success of a business organization in the industry. The volume of data collected is growing at an exponential rate, and the business needs to figure out a way to harness this data to create a competitive edge for itself. Information is subjected to timeliness. Obsolete or outdated information is of no use to the organization.

The sales manager has to think of ways on how the data can be used to improve business processes. It is not enough to have product knowledge; the value is in the application to the customer's processes. The value is generated by means of improvement in efficiency, effectiveness, and safety. Such improvements are reported by means of numbers once the data has been collected, processed, and turned into meaningful information.

There is an old saying: "A picture is worth a thousand words," so rather than always generating reports, graphical charts are better at communicating improvements in efficiency, effectiveness, and safety. This also applies to the presentations of case studies of customer-reference sites. The sales manager should also familiarize himself with statistical reports. Salespeople are very familiar with producing data in the form of a list. However, converting a data list into a two-dimensional table will enhance the presentation of the data.

Data is the fundamental building block for the development of business intelligence. The laying of the foundation for a strategy to gain competitive advantage has to be based on data. Likewise, a sales forecast has to be based on data. Product pricing has to be decided after crunching the historical data together with the sales forecast. Without data, it is merely guesswork, a gamble, "shooting into the air," etc.

For salesmanship, the objective of data collection, data structuring, data analysis, etc., for the sales manager is learning. What is the data telling us? In our economic world, most systems work with cyclical performances (e.g., financial markets, property markets, oil and gas markets, etc.) base on supply and demand. Out of the data analysis (which is not necessarily done by the sales manager), patterns are derived based on which decision on sales or marketing can be made.

The data kept by the organization in the form of a database, knowledge base, drawings database, etc., is the experience of the business.

35 Get a Customer, Keep a Customer

> Watch the little things; a small leak will sink a great ship.
>
> —Benjamin Franklin

Peter F. Drucker, one of the founders of management as a field of study, famously made the point that *"the purpose of a business is to create a customer."* Economic profit is the reward that markets bestow on those firms that succeed in this endeavour. Therefore, the function of a business is to "get a customer and keep a customer." This will ensure the survival of the business entity and sustainable growth. It is well documented in the business literature that getting a new customer is more costly than upselling and keeping an existing customer.

In order to keep the customer, it is important that customer satisfaction is protected. Therefore, the sales manager must periodically take the pulse of the customer's experience. This can be done by probing. Use open probes when you need to allow the customer to respond freely in order to gain general information or encourage further elaboration. Use closed probes when you need to limit the customer's response in order to uncover more specific information or confirm your understanding of the customer's statement or action.

When you recognize a customer's concern, express your awareness of the customer's concern and indicate what you plan to do next to address the concern and how it will help the customer. This is acknowledging the customer's concerns.

Informing is important when you need to report back on a service performed or make a recommendation or respond to a customer's request for information by stating the information including the what, why, and so forth. State the results the customer can expect, and determine the customer's acceptance/understanding.

Manage customer dissatisfaction (when the customer is dissatisfied) due to performance problems or unrealistic expectations or due to a misunderstanding. The first step is to acknowledge the customer's dissatisfaction. Inform the customer about whether your service can meet the expectations, and offer options when appropriate. When you have determined the customer's acceptance/understanding of your service or recommendation, review the commitments, if any, and indicate your availability for future service.

For ongoing customer maintenance (customer care), it is necessary that the sales manager keeps a close contact (customer touch point) with a planned schedule rather than leave it to ad hoc or chance visits due to a sales or service inquiry from the customer. Consistently showing up for the customer is the oil that lubricates the machinery of relationship and keeps the sales manager current with the developments of the customer.

A happy customer not only continues to give business but can also make a good sales reference. Further, there is a good chance that the sales manager can harness the customer's contacts (industry network) for new sales leads. Especially with "word of mouth" marketing, the more customers you have, the more contact and sales leads will be directed your way.

The sales manager has to keep vigilance on the performance of his technical, delivery, and other customer-facing teams. Any tardiness in the response to the customer, any lack of quality in the delivery or product, or any behavioral or unprofessional conduct is a sign or a red flag, and the sales manager needs to take immediate appropriate action. Some salespeople tend to adopt the attitude that once a sale is concluded, it is now the customer-service/care team that should be responsible and therefore held accountable if the customer is lost to the competition. In salesmanship practice, the sales manager is always the owner of the customer from the getting of the customer to the rest of the life cycle. Usually, once the customer is lost, it is nearly impossible to get the customer back. It is prudent not to leave the customer in others people's hands (i.e., technical team, delivery team, etc.) entirely as they may have a different set of KPIs or objectives. It is wise to avoid losing a customer in the first place when you still have control. It is like fixing a small leak that, if left unattended, over time may sink the ship.

36. Customer First

*The test of a first-rate intelligence is the ability to hold two opposing ideas
in mind at the same time and still retain the ability to function.*

—F. Scott Fitzgerald

Who comes first, the customer or the employee? This is a question that will oftentimes confront the sales manager, especially during sales cycles or the delivery process, when situations of conflict arise between the technical or delivery team and the customer's representative. Who should the sales manager stand with? If he takes the side of the customer, the internal team becomes unhappy. If he takes the side of the internal team, he risks losing the customer. As the old biblical saying goes, "no man can serve two masters."

Perhaps the oldest conundrum of all is this: which came first, the chicken or the egg? Similarly, the question to the sales manager is this: what comes first (in terms of importance), the customers or the employees (i.e., internal customers)?

On the one hand, as already mentioned earlier in chapter 35, Peter F. Drucker, one of the founders of management as a field of study, famously made the point that "the purpose of a business is to create a customer." The customer is the one paying for the services. For the sales manager, the idea is that we are in business to serve our customers, so they should be our primary focus. The premise is "No customer, no business."

On the other hand, employees meet customers during all those individual touch points along the end-to-end customer experience. As past experiences have shown, this places a great deal of stress on both the customers and employees. Customers want hassle-free, "Yes, sir" service from employees who are friendly and competent. Employees often want this as well, but the management wants to make a profit. This usually results in constraints on resources and time. However, the key distinction is that the business is paying the employees.

Rather than trying to decide where to put your ultimate focus, where to pin the sales strategy, and what to build as your biggest strength, it is best to find a balance between customer expectations and employee competency. If employees are not cared for, they cannot service the customers' expectations.

If customers are not served competently, then there is a risk of losing them. If customers are lost, employees will not have jobs. The employees who don't have jobs will move on. That means no resources will exist to serve the customer expectations. It is a spiral toward business failure.

This places the sales manager in a very difficult position. The company needs high-value customers above all if it is to be highly profitable. The top management expects strong quarter-upon-quarter profit growth even in a depressed market. In parallel, the company still needs to look after their best employees just as much as they look after their best customers. And if anything, the best employees are even harder to find. But businesses cannot put customers and employees first. Balancing employees and customers (i.e., profits) is a very hard job to do, especially when push comes to shove. One of them has to be given up first. It usually is not the profits.

We had a case where our key customer rejected our project manager on grounds that the project manager was deemed detrimental to the project's scope and success because he was always being emotional and saying no to the majority of requests from the customer's representative.

The customer representative always complained that they ended up doing quality assurance (i.e., test the software application and identifying bugs) when this should have been the supplier's responsibility. The project manager maintained that the so-called bugs were not bugs but the software running as designed and that the customer had just changed their mind again. The customer representative reported that the changes requested were not coming as speedily as the time schedule dictated. The project manager's view was that we were already working late hours and weekends.

In summary, the project manager was very vocal and opposed to the customer representative, and he said that they did not know what they wanted. To him, it seemed that the customer was the problem. The customer representative's view was that the project manager and team lacked the experience and competency to delivery such a project. It seemed like a blame game.

The truth is always somewhere in the middle of the two opposing views. Rather than spend too much time investigating who was right and who was wrong, we focused on the area that was under our direct control and causing the problem (i.e., the lack of domain knowledge and the quality assurance for our delivery process). We redeployed the project manager to another project to keep him happy.

We brought in a qualified domain expert to run the project and install an in-house quality-assurance engineer to arrest all the bugs before the delivery to the customer.

In conclusion, although we took an integrated approach to problem solving, we stayed with the salesmanship wisdom of "The customer comes first."

37. Sustainable Competitive Edge

> An organization's ability to learn, and translate that learning into
> action rapidly, is the ultimate competitive advantage.
>
> —Jack Welch

The eSET (enterprise survival equilateral triangle) model is based on the flight dynamics of airplanes. There are many similarities between keeping an airplane flying safely in the air and a business running in the face of intense competition. An airplane has three axes for flight coordination and control (i.e., ailerons [x-axis for roll], rudder [y-axis for yaw], and elevator [z-axis for pitch]). Similarly, in order for a business to fly well, there is a need to coordinate and control the three axes of an enterprise. See the figure below:

Fig. 7: Enterprise Survival Equilateral Triangle Model

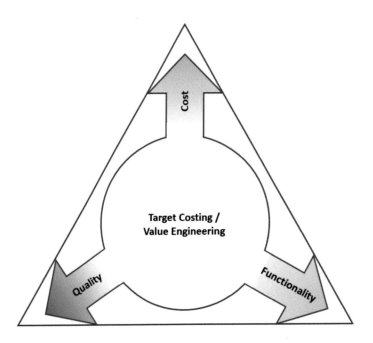

These three primary product/service-related characteristics play a crucial role in the success of a business entity, helping it sustain a competitive advantage and therefore survive. Most managers have failed to understand the role of the eSET model. The challenge is to balance the equilateral triangle as each of the primary characteristics is in conflict with the other two (e.g., if you try and reduce cost, a compromise on quality and/or functionality will become necessary).

From the customer's view of the three primary characteristics, he will only want to have the cost (which is translated into a price for him) reduced. He will want more of the quality and functionality at a given cost/price. This attempt at balancing the internal and customer views of the three primary characteristics will determine the enterprise's survival.

Internal View	Cost	Quality	Functionality
Customer View	Price	Perceived Quality	Perceived Functionality

38. Seven Deadly Sales Roadblocks

There are two kinds of pride, both good and bad. 'Good pride' represents our dignity and self-respect. 'Bad pride' is the deadly sin of superiority that reeks of conceit and arrogance.
—John C. Maxwell

The sales manager should decline to join a company where the CEO believes that he has no competition and sales will just happen. This is a red flag for the sales manager and a clear signal that the company is not market-oriented. When should a sales manager decide that it is time to move on? If any one or more of the seven deadly sales roadblocks exist, the sales manager should seriously make a decision on what he wants to do next.

Sales are a long-term endeavor and are built upon good relations with customers that are developed over time. However, if this cannot be achieved, then the sales manager is doomed to failure. The sales manager is not Superman; certain management decisions will affect the outcome of his sales effort. Therefore, he will always have to keep an eye on the environment that he is working in. Learning from history, there are seven deadly sales roadblocks that the sales manager should look out for:

1. *Primary Focus Is Profit:* This usually happens when the CEO has an accounting background and now runs the company or the company's majority-equity owner is an investment company. Purely focusing on the profit margin with no desire or interest in the products/services of the company is not a health sign for the sales manager. The company management does not take a long-term view of the business and will offload the company from the holding portfolio if an offer is made for its acquisition. In such a company, the employee morale is likely low and the delivery of product/service is also suffering. Customers buy because of the sales manager; his personal reputation is also at stake. The sales manager cannot be successful in such a situation as the future will always be uncertain. He should move on.

2. *Cost-Plus Pricing:* The company's pricing policy is internal-looking, not market-oriented. Closely related to sales roadblock number 1 is cost-plus pricing. The Western suppliers (i.e., American and European groups) practice this method of pricing (i.e., calculate the cost [usually in their respective countries with high costs] and add a margin on top). This usually results in a price that is not competitive in the market, especially with Asian makers making similar products that have today's good quality standards of products made in Asia. Once the product is released to the market, price cuts are necessary for sales to happen. This puts the product back on the design table for a redesign to reduce the product cost. Asian companies practice target-cost pricing to support the early-design stage, targeting the cost by using value engineering (VE), industrial engineering, and simplification methods to focus on cost reduction and waste elimination. The sales manager will never be successful with a cost-plus-pricing policy, and he should move on.

3. *Market Myopia:* This is the subordination of a new business to an old cash-cow business. Some companies continue the sale of an older model or older product when a new product is already available to be pushed into the market. The production cost of the old product continues beyond the product's life cycle, and after-sales obligations continue to hold back the company from capturing the new product market. In the meantime, the competition takes a great part of the market share. This is a sign of weak top management and a lack of willingness to make a clear decision. The sales manager is better off moving on.

4. *Sales Disconnect with Delivery:* When products are rolled out fast and furiously, the 7 Ps (product, price, package, promotion, place, people, and positioning) are not applied. Problem solving (i.e., damage containment) becomes the focus, and new opportunities are neglected. This situation does not have clear release strategies—a result of the push to meet sales numbers to recover the investment in product development or deal with cash-flow problems. This situation does not have the right people with the

domain knowledge on product development and deployment. This is a sign of a clear disconnect between the top management's strategy and the development and delivery teams' directions and actions. It is unlikely that this situation will improve any time soon. The sales manager should move on.

5. *Staying in Comfort Zone:* Western companies, mainly American and European ones, refuse to provide a complete solution from one source. Western managers are risk-averse and will shy away if a customer would like a one-stop solution. In my past European company, we would sit by and lose a deal but would not agree to take the ownership for the complete project because our portion of the deal was smaller than that of our subcontractor. We consistently lost the deals to Asian companies, especially if there was no local support and the sales manager had to await support from Europe (which involved a time difference and language barrier). It is unlikely the sales manager can be successful with such poor back-end support. The sales manager is justified to move on.

6. *Not Customer-Oriented:* Although I learned the concept of being customer-oriented from a Western management school, in the industry, it is the Asian companies that are customer-oriented. To gain a competitive edge in the market, a company can rely on things like pricing, innovation, or image. But one of the most effective ways of standing out from the rest is to offer quality service that meets customer expectations. This will also boost the image of the company. Being customer-oriented requires a long-term strategy that should involve the whole company—from the top management to the grassroots staff. It also means a change of mentality and an internal organization that trains its sights on a new target: satisfying customer expectations. In my past company, our Western managers were always hostile to the requests of our customer representatives. Any request would be met with a no first, almost to the point of treating a customer as an enemy. Another common response was "Oh, we have to charge for this" before the customer even finished with his request. It was always confrontational, and instead of a win-win situation, the goal was always that we would win while the customer lost. The sales manager should run fast; no need for a second opinion.

7. *Cronyism:* The management does not value the principle of meritocracy, putting people in charge even if they are without the qualifications and experiences needed to be effective in their roles. They protect team members who are not performing and are in positions not based on their own merits. In such a working environment, the sales manager will usually be caught between the customer and delivery team. Consequently, the result is poor service and poor customer relations. The sales manager should move on at the earliest opportunity.

39. Ethics in Sales

> I don't want to do anything that violates my own personal code of ethics and morals.
>
> —Michael Moore

The salesmanship code of conduct is one of *respect for the law, service to the customer, fellowship with colleagues*, and *never underestimating the competition*. For the sales manager, these qualities are essential. These qualities will prevent anyone from enticing the sales manager into unsuitable places where he may be suddenly confronted with awkward situations, and thus the sales manager can avoid running afoul of the law and the resulting calamities.

Respect for the law guides the sales manager on what is right and what is wrong. Acting rightly and doing good are difficult and are regarded as tiresome, whereas acting wrongly is easy and amusing. This may be due to a lack of capacity for self-control. Though it may not sound so bad, if we examine its origin, we will find that it arises from cowardice. Right conduct means doing deeds of outstanding merit, moderating one's appetite for eating and drinking, and avoiding the overindulgence of sex, which is the greatest delusion of mankind, so that one may preserve one's body's health and strength.

Filial duty requires that one's conduct is correct in all points. For if there is no discrimination in all matters, there will be no knowledge of what is right. Therefore, the sales manager must be very diligent to study whenever there is any spare time so as to gain a thorough knowledge of sales, marketing, product specifications, etc., for both study and practice are necessary for one to excel in sales.

Correct etiquette and manners by which respect is shown to customers and fellow team members should also be observed by the sales manager. The sales manager must always practice thrift and have the discrimination to do it so the company will not have a deficit in its accounts (budget). It is financial difficulty that induces even those with a high reputation to do dishonest things—things that are quite alien to them. So one must make a firm resolve to live according to one's means and be very careful not to indulge in any useless expenses, spending money only when it is necessary. However, there is a need for balance. Flipping over to unusual or excessive frugality or stinginess is also not acceptable. That is why in old China, *parsimony* was regarded as synonymous with *cowardice*.

"A hawk may be starving but it will not touch corn." It is a sense of shame or pride, and the sales manager, like the hawk, must not compromise his morals and ethics. This means that it is also important for the sales manager to choose which friends he keeps. He must stay away from braggarts and slanderers. Everything that comes out of the sales manager's mouth must be considered and guarded. It is essential to think carefully before one speaks, for it is out of words that disputes arise. For a sales manager, a handshake is like a verbal contract.

The sales manager should not engage in frivolous arguments/discussions. However, if he does become a party of such a discussion, it will be most helpful if he states what he thinks clearly and succinctly—without reserve and without any regard for the disapproval or resentment others may show. For if he exhibits a maladroit hesitancy and turns aside from what is just and agrees with what is not reasonable out of weakness or fear of opposing people or offending them, his act will be an injustice.

Again the sales manager should not be so stupid as to think of himself too much of a personage to take part in a confabulation, arguing that there is no need for consultation and wishing to decide everything according to his own opinion and so make a mess of things and become unpopular among his fellows.

Below is a summary in point form of what the sales manager *must not do—even with the blessing or direction of his superiors*:

a) Corruption (i.e., give or receive bribes or favors)
b) Con schemes, cheating, and misleading
c) Overselling the products or services
d) Being too emotional or displaying one's feelings openly
e) Breaking off sales contracts or failing to deliver
f) Discrediting the reputation of the company or products/services
g) Creative accounting (i.e., invoice generation for nonsales)
h) Making side deals (i.e., agreeing to payment terms other than those documented)
i) Using company time for nonsales activities (e.g., fictitious sales visits)
j) Freely sharing the company's confidential data with the competition (e.g., prices)
k) Excessive eating, drinking, gambling, and sex

l) Procrastination and laziness

m) Flip-flop on your commitments

n) Bragging, bad-mouthing, or politicking

o) Blaming others or giving excuses for everything or reasons why something cannot be done

p) Getting into conflicts of interest with the company's business

q) Moonlighting or engaging in other endeavors

r) Being argumentative or aggressive

s) Telling lies or half-truths

"Alright, who folded the printout into a paper airplane?"

40. Conclusion

Our only security is our ability to change.

—John Lilly

This text is about collaborative salesmanship (i.e., turning customer requirements into revenue by adding value to the customer's processes). In the information age, sales has been transformed from a transactional type (i.e., buyer-and-seller relationship) to a collaboration between different individuals and different entities brought about by supply-chain interaction and the fulfillment of needs driven by intense competition in the industry.

All efforts in adding value to the customer's processes come down to driving the efficiency and/or effectiveness of the organization. This means that collaborative salesmanship can finally either target to save cost (i.e., efficiency) or increase revenue (i.e., effectiveness) or both. Likewise, this collaborative salesmanship can also be applied to the people, products, and services of an organization.

This shift in the way sales take place has also led to the change in the sales-manager profile. In order to be able to conduct business in the information age, the sales manager needs additional skills that will enable him to perform this new role. In this engagement model, he is both the consultant on one hand (i.e., learning from others in the market and sharing these ideas with the customer) and the facilitator on the other hand (i.e., providing the enablement tools and support to get the customer started).

This shift in sales has also led to changes in the sales cycle. During the former times, a few visits to a customer for the conduction of discussions and negotiations would have resulted in the conclusion of a sale. Now the engagement process usually starts with a trial implementation of the proposed solution, and this can last up to six months. The results of the trial will determine the success of the sale of the proposal for adoption by the customer.

To ensure that the trial will be successful, the sales manager needs to understand the expectations of the different stakeholders. He has to start with the objectives and the measures to be applied in the calibration of the trial's report and lesson. Data collection and analysis become important aspects of the trial. Understanding and interpreting the data become crucial in the determination of the trial's progress and outcome. Good data is half the battle won. Bad or missing data can spell trouble for the sales cycle.

Communication and the way progress is reported to the different stakeholders cannot be left to chance. The C-level stakeholders would like to have dashboards and "what if" simulations for decision support (i.e., preprocessed information ready for consumption). The operational- and technical-management teams need to be able to review the somewhat raw data and perform the analysis of data that feeds up to the dashboards and "what if" simulations. It is here that the sales manager's roles of consultant and facilitator become obvious.

Appendix A: Sales-Process Flow

If you cannot describe what you are doing as a process, you do not know what you are doing.

—W. Edwards Deming

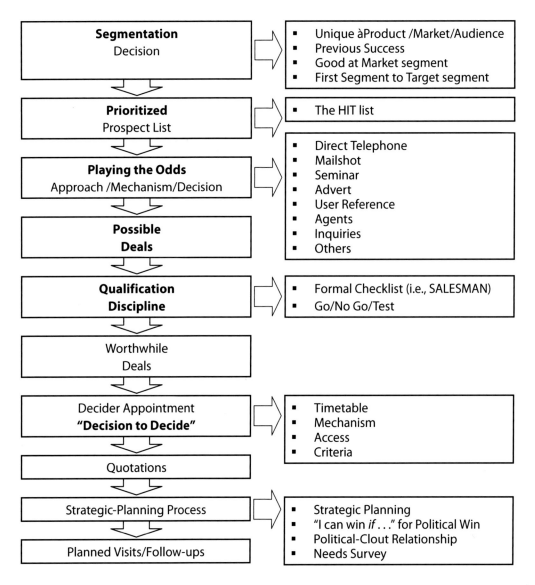

Segmentation
Decision
- Unique àProduct /Market/Audience
- Previous Success
- Good at Market segment
- First Segment to Target segment

Prioritized
Prospect List
- The HIT list

Playing the Odds
Approach /Mechanism/Decision
- Direct Telephone
- Mailshot
- Seminar
- Advert
- User Reference
- Agents
- Inquiries
- Others

Possible
Deals

Qualification
Discipline
- Formal Checklist (i.e., SALESMAN)
- Go/No Go/Test

Worthwhile
Deals

Decider Appointment
"Decision to Decide"
- Timetable
- Mechanism
- Access
- Criteria

Quotations

Strategic-Planning Process
- Strategic Planning
- "I can win *if* . . ." for Political Win
- Political-Clout Relationship
- Needs Survey

Planned Visits/Follow-ups

Appendix B: Breaking into the Account

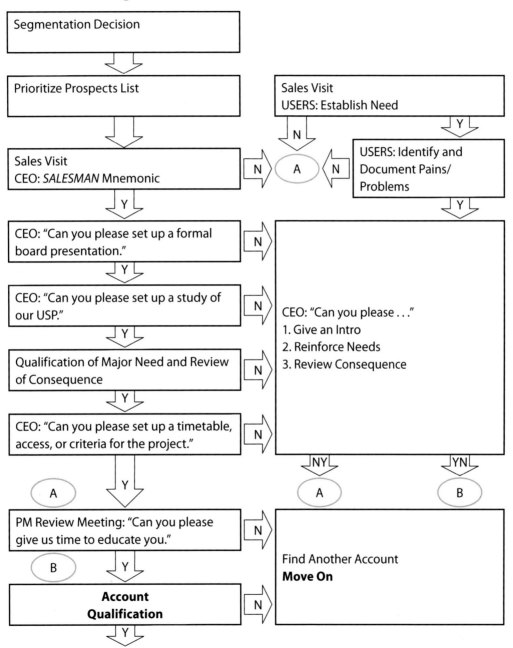

Appendix C: Solution to Exercise in Chapter 16

Please try and solve this puzzle. How would you make the line A—A¹ shorter without touching the line?

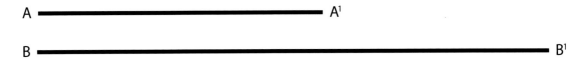

Line A—A¹ is made shorter by placing a longer line, called B—B¹, next to it.
This way, you will never have to touch the line A—A¹.

The purpose of the above exercise is to illustrate that the sales manager can focus on things under his control and achieve a competitive advantage by amplifying his own company/product/service/ solution strengths and thereby making the competitors' offers shorter by perception in relative terms in the mind of the customer.

Appendix D: Sales Cycles, Criteria, and Concerns

In sales, it is not what you say; it is how they perceive what you say

—Jeffrey Gitomer

The sales manager cannot simply and directly apply in the field, what is learned from this book. Salesmanship is not a definitive field of science like medicine, botany, geology, etc. It is a social science and guided by the behavioral patterns of customers in specific industries. Therefore, the application has to be adopted on a case to case basis, with no two customers behaving in the same way, especially for B2B (Business to Business) sales.

In the practice of salesmanship, it is important to appreciate that depending on where you are in the sales cycle, the likelihood of the criteria for evaluation of the solution and the level of customer concerns will be shifting in importance. This knowledge is fundamental for the development of sales strategies for managing accounts and acquisition of new customers.

"After-sales service" is an important aspect of *value* for the customer that usually appears on the agenda just before the customer makes a commitment to purchase. The sales manager must think not only about product FAB (features and benefits); this is well and good for the customer evaluation process for the comparison to other competitive products. However, what the sales manager really needs to do is talk about *insights*, e.g., what is the cost of error, cost of delay, and cost of failure? Usually the customer will underestimate the cost and consequence of such error, delay, or failure. This is the *provocation* the sales manager needs to instigate the customer to act, with a sense of urgency.

When developing a sales strategy for a particular customer, the sales manager should ask himself such questions: Why should the customer buy now? Why from us? Why our solutions? What is the *value* to the customer of our services network, documentation, our help desk support, our product upgrade release program, etc.? The sales manager has to be mindful that operational managers may not see the value being proposed because at his level, he may not see the big picture, as cost (of error, delay, or failure) sometimes get passed downstream in the supply chain and shows up somewhere else from the origin (root cost). In such cases, the sales manager must have the confidence to move up the organization hierarchy to lobby his case.

Let us revisit the sales cycle, see figure below. The typical stages of the sales cycle are Identify, Evaluation, Solution-selling, Decision-making, and Project start. Of course, you can rename the stages or even expand the stages but these five stages are sufficient for our discussion here. Now having established the typical sales cycle, we can start to map the customer's perspective, the supplier's view, and the sales manager's insight to the typical sales cycle stages. Having done this, the sales manager can now "operationalize" his sales strategy into an action plan.

SALES CYCLE

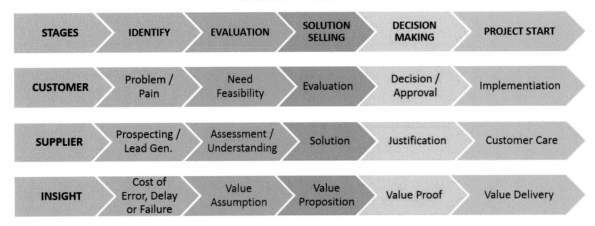

STAGES	IDENTIFY	EVALUATION	SOLUTION SELLING	DECISION MAKING	PROJECT START
CUSTOMER	Problem / Pain	Need Feasibility	Evaluation	Decision / Approval	Implementiation
SUPPLIER	Prospecting / Lead Gen.	Assessment / Understanding	Solution	Justification	Customer Care
INSIGHT	Cost of Error, Delay or Failure	Value Assumption	Value Proposition	Value Proof	Value Delivery

During the Identify stage of the sales cycle, the sales manager is engaged in *prospecting* for sales leads.

As the sale progresses to the Evaluation stage, the sales manager starts to build a picture of the prospects in terms of people, potential for the project, and starts to confirm the need.

Then the next stage is Solution-selling. Here the sales manager focuses on positioning a *unique solution* for the prospect, starts to firm up what to sell and why. He studies the competition's involvement in the account—since when and why. Demo the product FAB (features and benefits). Start presentations on the "how" of the project, which will be executed in terms of technical and commercial aspects.

At the Decision-making stage, the sales manager's efforts are focused on closing the deal. The sales manager provides evidence on *meeting the needs* and *delivery of value,* sales manager's CEO visit to call "higher-ups" in the customer organization, referrals, and site visit for proof of quality service delivery including after-sales support network.

Of course, in reality the sales cycle stages are not so clear cut.

Now that we have a somewhat deeper understanding of the sales cycle stages, we can begin to build the correlation of the customer's "level of concern" to the key selection criteria for the purchase. The same criteria will shift in level of concern or importance as the sales progresses through the sales cycle stages. See figure below on Level of Concern vs. Criteria.

During the Identify stage, the sales manager is prospecting for sales leads. Price (cost), product (FAB), and value are the key criteria the customer is using to invite/select the suppliers.

As the sales progresses to the Evaluation stage, the product (FAB), value, and urgency (i.e., product delivery date, lead time, etc.) grows in importance. Price (cost) is being postponed to later stage of the sales cycle for commercial discussion. "Technical" compliance takes precedence in the short listing of the product/vendor.

Than the next stage is Solution-selling, here is where the sales manager conducts a demonstration of his solution, provide insights specific to the prospect and make propositions on value to be gained from the implementation.

At the Decision-making stage, the customer's senior management steps into the project decision-making resulting in a shift of the level of concern of the selection criteria. Value (insight), urgency, risk (evaluation of company commercials standing, credit worthiness, management team, etc.) and after-sales support network take precedence in the project award. Price (cost) will be negotiated after selection, is a usual industry practice before the final contract award. Product (FAB) is no longer the key concern by this stage of the sale cycle.

Level of Concern vs. Criteria

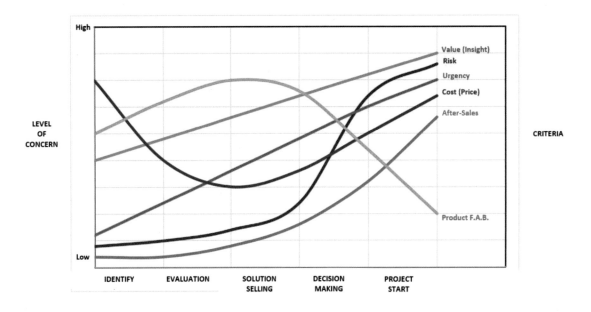

Is it enough that the sales manager gains a good understanding about what needs to be the focus during the different stages of the sales cycle. What about *conflict* in the sales cycle? The sales manager can avoid conflict between sales vs. delivery team (i.e., engineering, production, logistics, etc.) if attention is paid to the "scope" of delivery in terms of what needs to be delivered, when, in what quantity and where? If attention can be paid to these questions early in the sales cycle, with proper communication and documentation, there is a good chance than, the usual fight between sales vs. delivery can be avoided.

Usually the root cause of the conflict between sales vs. delivery can be beyond the influence of the sales manager. Therefore, senior management has to actively participate in resolving the potential conflict before it happens.

Appendix E: Sales Trials, MoU's, and Handshakes

Experience teaches you that the man who looks you straight in the eye,
particularly if he adds a firm handshake, is hiding something

—Clifton Fadiman

Sales trials are an excellent way of engaging a customer to gain an insight of a product's functionality and benefits (FAB). However, the trial should be planned with a single point of contact both from the customer's side and the sales manager's side. Clear objectives for the trial should be documented and signed by both parties in the form of a memorandum of understanding (MoU). Although an MoU is not a legally binding document, it is a great way to move the deal forward and avoid any misunderstanding on all parties involved. The MoU should clarify the project charter, objectives, duration, roles and responsibilities, etc. That is, once the objectives are met, the customer is obliged to progress with the sales and implementation.

So is a handshake enough for a trial instead of writing up a MoU, a handshake instead of a sales contract. Or is handshake enough to ignore all the terms and conditions in a contract and proceed with the sale? Myself included, there are many instances where sales managers eager to close a deal will start work on the project even before a proper sales contract is signed. This can be *a leap of faith* as sales managers are usually risk takers. This can also be a case where during the sales cycle, a relationship has developed and the sales manager *trusts* the customer and truly believes that all is good to start the project or deliver the goods.

Actually, I am quite an optimistic person. But nevertheless, I would strictly enforce that "no paper, no delivery" rule. This is based on past experiences. Trust and handshake is all good; however, it is not legally binding. Even if you run your own business (as an entrepreneur), you should restrain yourselves from the practice of doing business only on a handshake. The paperwork must be put in place at the earliest opportunity. The reason is simple: a handshake is a contract based on "honor." Only a person who exercises value character will honor his words. Most mortals will experience some kind of a "purchase dissonance" and can virtually back out of the *handshake contract* for a variety of excuses, such as the person leaves the customer organization, he resigns, the project budget gets cancelled, etc. When this happens, the salesman has no recourse to legal means. You will need a sales contract or some form of commitment in written form to enforce payment or exercise your legal rights. Verbal agreements and handshakes are not legally binding.

There are many cases, when verbal or handshake agreements are cancelled. In this case, the sales manager will not only lose the sale but would have, in the meantime, incur real cost. Such cost could wipe out the profits gained from previous deals closed by the sales manager. Therefore, it is prudent that the sales manager does not simply rely on a handshake, and this is applicable in the world globally, not just in Asia.

Bibliography

The best advice I ever got was that knowledge is power and to keep reading.

—David Bailey

These are books that I have read and that shaped my thoughts on salesmanship. I would recommend this as a reading list for the salesmanship practitioner.

Marketing / Customer Relationship Management (CRM)

Anton, Jon. *Customer Relationship Management: Making Hard Decisions with Soft Numbers.* New Jersey: Prentice-Hall, 1996.

Johansson, Johnny K., and Ikujiro Nonaka. *Relentless: The Japanese Way of Marketing.* Oxford: Butterworth-Heinemann, 1996.

Page, Rick. *Hope Is Not a Strategy: The 6 Keys to Winning the Complex Sale.* Atlanta: Nautilus Press Inc., 2002.

Supply Chain (SCM)

Bolstorf, Peter, and Robert Rosenbaum. *Supply Chain Excellence: A Handbook for Dramatic Improvement Using the SCOR Model.* New York: AMACOM, 2003.

Rachan, Wilfred. *The Effects of Collaborative Supply Chain Solutions on Strategic Performance Management.* Netherlands: Leiden University Press, 2012.

Management, Leadership, and Personal Development (HRM)

Carnegie, Dale. *How to Win Friends & Influence People.* New York: Gallery Books, 1981.

Chu, Ching Ning. *The Asian Mind Game.* New York: Macmillan Publishing Company, 1991.

Clampitt, P. G. *Communicating for Managerial Effectiveness*. California: Sage Publications Inc., 2004.

Covey, Stephen R. *The 7 Habits of Highly Effective People*. New York: FIRESIDE, 1989.

Connelly, Richard, Robin McNeill, and Roland Mosimann. *The Multidimensional Manager*. Ottawa: Cognos, 1996.

De Bono, Edward. *Textbook of Wisdom*. London: Penguin, 1997.

Goldratt, E. M., and J. Cox. *The Goal: A Process of Ongoing Improvement*. Great Barrington, Massachusetts: North River Press, 1986.

Harris, L. C., and E. Ogbonna. "Leadership Style and Market Orientation: An Empirical Study." *European Journal of Marketing* 35(5) (2001): 744–764.

Josserand, E. *The Network Organization: The Experience of Leading French Multinationals*. Cheltenham, United Kingdom: Edward Elgar Publishing Ltd., 2004.

Mercer, David. *IBM: How the World's Most Successful Corporation Is Managed*. London: Kogan Page, 1987.

Action Learning (AL)

Coghlan, D., T. Dromgoole, P. Joynt, and P. Sorensen. *Managers Learning in Action: Management Learning, Research and Education*. London: Routledge, 2004.

Coutu, D. L. "Anxiety of Learning." *Harvard Business Review* 80(3) (2002): 100–108.

Cunningham, I., B. Bennett, and G. Dawes. *Self-Managed Learning in Action: Putting SML into Practice*. England: Gower Publishing Ltd., 2000.

Novak, J. D., and D. B. Gowin. *Learning to Learn*. Cambridge, United Kingdom: Cambridge University Press, 1984.

Society and Economics

Doukidis, G. I., N. Mylonopoulos, and N. Pouloudi. *Social and Economic Transformation in the Digital Era*. Hershey, Pennsylvania: Idea Group Inc., 2003.

Friedman, George. *The Next 100 Years*. London: Allison & Busby Ltd., 2009.

Gore, Albert, Jr. *The Future: Six Drivers of Global Change*. New York: Random House, 2013.

Grant, J. L. *Foundations of Economic Value Added*. New Jersey: John Wiley & Sons, 2003.

Samuel, Y. *The Political Agenda of Organizations*. New Brunswick, New Jersey: Transaction Publisher, 2005.

Vygotsky, L. S. *Mind and Society: The Development of Higher Mental Processes*. Cambridge, Massachusetts: Harvard University Press, 1978.

Quality Assurance (QA) / Production Management

Fairfield-Sonn, James W. *Corporate Culture and the Quality Organization*. Westport, Connecticut: Greenwood Publishing, 2000.

Imai, M. *Gemba Kaizen: A Common Sense, Low-Cost Approach to Management*. New York: McGraw-Hill Inc., 1997.

Souchkov, Valeri. *TRIZ: The Right Solution at the Right Time*. Netherlands: Insytec BV, 1999.

Information Technology (IT)

Gates, Bill. "Business @ the Speed of Thought: Using a Digital Nervous System." *Information Management Journal* 34(3) (2000): 50–52.

Gerste, Robert. *The Guide to Knowledge-Based Improvement*. Calgary: Converge Consulting Group Inc., 2001.

Goldratt, E. M. *Haystack Syndrome*. Great Barrington, Massachusetts: North River Press, 1990.

Luftman, J. N. *Competing in the Information Age: Align in the Sand*. New York: Oxford University Press, 2003.

Strategy

Koufteros, X. A., M. A. Vonderembse, and W. J. Doll. "Integrated Product Development Practice and Competitive Capabilities: The Effects of Uncertainty, Equivocality and Platform Strategy." *Journal of Operations Management* 20(4) (2002): 331–335.

Porter, M. E. *Competitive Advantage*. New York: The Free Press, 1985.

Porter, M. E. "What Is Strategy?" *Harvard Business Review* (Nov.–Dec. 1996): 61–78.

Sales Management / Selling

Freese, Thomas. *Secrets of Question Based Selling: How the Most Powerful Tool in Business Can Double Your Sales Results*. Naperville: Sourcebooks Inc., 2000.

Rosen, Keith. *The Complete Idiot's Guide to Cold Calling*. New York: Penguin, 2004.

Beckwith, Harry. *Selling the Invisible: A Field Guide to Modern Marketing*. New York: Warner Books Inc., 1997.

Tracy, Brian. *The Psychology of Selling*. Nashville: Thomas Nelson, 2004.

Ziglar, Zig. *Secrets of Closing the Sale*. Michigan: Revell, 2004.

Finance and Accounting

Fields, E. *Essentials of Finance and Accounting for Nonfinancial Managers*. New York: AMACOM Division, American Management Association, 2002.

Printed in the United States
By Bookmasters